D0677094

Legal Almanac Series No. 13

CIVIL LIBERTY AND CIVIL RIGHTS

by **Edwin S. Newman**

*This legal Almanac has been revised
by the Oceana Editorial Staff*

Irving J. Sloan
General Editor

SIXTH EDITION

1979 Oceana Publications, Inc.
Dobbs Ferry, New York

KF4750
.N44
1978

Library of Congress Cataloging in Publication Data

Newman, Edwin S.
  Civil liberty and civil rights.

  (Legal almanac series; no. 13)
  1. Civil rights--United States--Popular works.
I. Title.
KF4750.N44   1978   342'.73'085   78-12034
ISBN 0-379-11110-1

© Copyright 1979 by Oceana Publications, Inc.

All rights reserved. No part of this publication may be repro-
duced or transmitted in any form or by any means, electronic or
mechanical, including photocopy, recording, xerography, or
any information storage and retrieval system, without per-
mission in writing from the publisher.

Manufactured in the United States of America.

550

TABLE OF CONTENTS

INTRODUCTION v

Chapter I
FIRST AMENDMENT RIGHTS 1
  I. Religious Freedom 1
  II. Other First Amendment Issues 11

Chapter II
GUARANTEES OF PERSONAL LIBERTY 47

Chapter III
SUMMARY OF THE PRIVACY ACT OF 1974 71

Chapter IV
CIVIL RIGHTS 81
  I. The Role of the Federal Government 81
  II. The States and Civil Rights 93

Appendix
CONSTITUTIONAL AMENDMENTS 115

INDEX 121

INTRODUCTION

Civil Liberties and Civil Rights

Definition and Distinction

When our founding fathers made us one nation, they had this fear--that a strong central government might overrun the rights of the people. To prevent this, they drew up a list of prohibitions on the powers of the federal government. No religion was to be established; the people were to enjoy freedom of speech, press assembly and religious worship; a man's life, liberty, and property were to be protected against arbitrary action by the government. These prohibitions, securing freedom of expression and the protection of personal liberty, were set down in the Bill of Rights, the first ten amendments to the Constitution.

Initially, these prohibitions were directed only against the federal government. The respective states, however, in their own constitutions, adopted similar prohibitions protecting the liberty of the people against arbitrary action by state government. Then, after the Civil War, the Fourteenth Amendment to the Constitution was passed. Under this amendment, no state could deprive any person of life, liberty or property without due process of law. Gradually, this "due process" clause of the Fourteenth Amendment came to include most of the prohibitions of the Bill of Rights, so that the Constitution became complete protection for the people against the action of both state and federal government. These rights, protected by the Bill of Rights and by the Fourteenth Amendment, are known as our "civil liberties."

Specifically, they include the requirement that Church and State be separated; the freedom of speech, press, assembly and religion; protection against double jeopardy; the right not to be a witness against one's self; protection against unreasonable searches and seizures and against excessive fines and punishments; the right to counsel in criminal cases; and the right to trial by jury. Of course, the exercise of these rights is not absolute; nor is the extent of protection always the same regardless of whether a state or the federal government is involved.

It is one thing, however, to protect the people against the government; it is quite another to protect them against themselves. While the founding fathers dealt wisely with the possibility of tyranny by government, it was only through trial and error experience that we came gradually to deal with the problem of the tyranny of the majority.

Under the Constitution, the government should not act to quiet an unpopular viewpoint; but there was little to stand in the way of a mob riding a man out of town because he spoke his mind. Under the Constitution, the government could not act to establish any one religion; yet, there are pages of our history which tell of unpunished burnings of churches, libel and slander against members of minority religious groups and incitement to violence against them. Under the Constitution, the government could not reduce any American to second-class citizenship because of the color of his skin or his racial origin; intolerance, however, created discrimination against colored persons, and in some instances, the outright threat to their lives, liberty and property.

Over the past hundred years, this problem of the protection of the people from one another has come to be dealt with in an increasingly effective and successful way--through a combination of amendments to the federal Constitution, through state and federal legislation, and perhaps, most significantly, through the courts, and in particular, the United States Supreme Court. The rights thus created, designed to protect the equal standing of the individual before his government, but primarily to protect the freedom of the individual against attacks by other persons, are known as our "civil rights."

Chapter I
FIRST AMENDMENT RIGHTS

Religious Freedom

This nation was founded by people who had fled from the religious persecutions and intolerance of seventeenth and eighteenth century Europe. They sought and found on these shores the opportunity to worship according to the dictates of their conscience. But many of these people refused to extend to others the freedoms they found for themselves. Religious toleration did not prevail in the colonies which they had established. In fact, they excluded from their colonies persons of other religious beliefs or severely punished dissenters from the religion of the majority. This policy proved impractical and by the time of the American Revolutionary War the colonies had relaxed most of their restraints on worship and permitted members of all faiths to pursue their own religious beliefs and practices. By the time the Constitution was drawn up, our leading statesmen had become tolerant.

One cannot argue, however, that those who wrote our Constitution were hostile to religion, or that they believed that there should be no relationship whatsoever between the federal government and the churches. Nevertheless, whatever the individual feelings might have been among the writers of that document, they clearly agreed that the functions of government and religion should be completely separate. Religion and government as institutions would be best served, they felt, if neither tried to exert its influence over the policies of the other.

The First Amendment is the foundation stone of religious liberty in the United States. This Amendment provides that "Congress shall make no law respecting an establishment of religion, or prohibiting the free exercise thereof. . . ." Essentially, this means that (1) Congress -- and under the Fourteenth Amendment, the legislatures of the states -- must not assist or finance one "official" religion, since that would be an "establishment" specifically prohibited by the First Amendment, and (2) that there must be no legal requirements or penalties governing what a person should believe, or the manner in which a person should worship.

It is the First Amendment which is the basis for all areas of religious freedom. However, it should be noted that there exists in the body of the Constitution an important provision dealing directly with a crucial religious right, the forbidding of religious tests as qualifications for public office.

Another important point about the "religion clause" is that it is confined the inherent prohibitions against governmental action to the federal government. At the time of the adoption of the Constitution of the United States many of the original thirteen states had specific religious establishments or other restrictive provisos. Indeed, in these earliest days of the Republic, only Virginia and Rhode Island had conceded full, unqualified freedom. By 1833, however, following the capitulation of the Congregationalists in Massachusetts, the fundamental concepts of freedom of religion had, to all intents and purposes, become a recognized fact and facet of public law, with only minor aberrations, throughout the young nation.

One of the problems in the interpretation of the religion clause is that its language speaks both of the "establishment" of religion and the "free exercise" of religion. It was not until the New Jersey Bus case (1947) that the Court held that the First Amendment's prohibition against legislation respecting an establishment of religion is also applicable to the several states by virtue of the language and obligations of the Fourteenth Amendment. Thus not until 1947 had both aspects of the religion guarantee been judicially interpreted to apply to both the federal government and the states.

The classic definition of "religion" was given by the Supreme Court in 1890 when the Court unanimously upheld a lower court judgment that one Samuel Davis, a Mormon residing in the then Territory of Idaho, should be disqualified as voter for falsifying his voter's oath "abjuring bigamy or polygamy as a condition to vote" since, as a Mormon, he believed in polygamy. Polygamy, then as now a criminal offense, constituted a disqualification under territorial voting and other statutes. Mr. Justice Stephen Field wrote for the Court:

> The term "religion has reference to one's view of
> his relations to his creator, and to the obligations
> they impose of reverence for his being and character,

and of obedience to his will. It is often confounded with the cultus or form of worship of a particular sect, but is distinguishable from the latter. . . . With man's relations to his Maker and the obligations he may think they impose, and the manner in which an expression shall be made by him of his belief on those subjects, no interference can be permitted, provided always the laws of society, designed to secure its peace and prosperity, and the morals of its people are not interfered with. . . .

Thus, although giving religion the widest feasible interpretation in terms of individual commitment, Field found that Davis had violated the reservation of the last qualifying clause.

As the years passed, this Supreme Court definition of religion was most often tested in cases dealing with military exemptions and conscientious objectors. Exemption from the draft and/or combat service for those who oppose war on religious grounds is deeply rooted in American tradition and history -- although it was not really institutionalized until post-Civil War years. Much litigation has attended this problem, frequently involving the Jehovah's Witnesses, who contend that every believing Witness is a "minister" and as such ought to be exempt from military service. Both the Quakers (Society of Friends) and the Mennonites have made pacifism a dogma. And of course there has been a perpetual stream of individual conscientious objectors coming from small Protestant sects as well as from other faiths. The Vietnam War was a period of large numbers of objectors. Congress has always recognized bona fide conscientious objectors and exempting them from military service. But it is not clear that there exists a constitutional rather than a moral obligation to exempt conscientious objectors.

The Vietnam War raised the question of whether an individual may qualify as a conscientious objector because his or her belief dictates against participation in a particular war but not against participation in all wars. In 1971 the Supreme Court heard the arguments of two such objectors, one whose belief was "based on a humanist approach to religion," and the other, a devout Catholic, who believed it his duty according to his religion "to discriminate between 'just' and 'unjust' wars, and to foreswear participation in the latter." The petitioners based their argument on two grounds: first, that exemption of only those individuals whose belief dictates against participation in all wars acts as an establishment of religion in that it excludes

3

those religions which require the individual to differentiate between just and unjust war; and second, that the exemption interferes with the free exercise of religion of those who wish to make that differentiation. The Court rejected both arguments, holding that here the government's interest in fairly determining who is required to serve in the armed forces outweighs the claims of individual conscience. The problems of determining what might constitute legitimate objection to a particular war are so great, declared the Court, as to be incapable of fair determination. Such objection might be largely political in nature, or it might be subject to change and nullification during the course of a particular war. Finally, the recognition of selective rather than general conscientious objection might well "open the doors to a general theory of selective disobedience to law." and could well pose a serious threat to the morale and resolve of one whose objection to a particular war might be equally strong as that of the conscientious objector but who based that objection on political or moral rather than religious grounds." It does not bespeak an establishing of religion for Congress to forego the enterprise of distinguishing those whose dissent has some conscientious bases from those who simply dissent," concluded the Court.

Before leaving the religious clause of the First Amendment, a discussion of the subject of its prohibitions in relationship to public education.

Few judicial decisions have produced more violent controversy than the Supreme Court's ruling in the Regents' Prayer case (Engel v. Vitale).

On June 25, 1962, the Court held 6-1 that the 22-word prayer adopted by the New York State Board of Regents in 1951 was

"wholly inconsistent with the Establishment Clause" of the First Amendment. The prayer read: "Almighty God, we acknowledge our dependence upon Thee, and we beg Thy blessing upon us, our parents, our teachers and our country."

Writing for the majority, Justice Hugo L. Black said:

" . . . The First Amendment was added to the Constitution . . . as a guarantee that neither the power nor the prestige of the Federal Government would be used to control, support, or influence the kinds of prayer the American people can say . . . .

4

It is no part of the business of government to compose official prayers for any group . . . to recite as part of a religious program carried on by the government . . . . Neither the fact that the prayer may be denominationally neutral, nor . . . that its observance . . . is voluntary can serve to free it from the limitations of the Establishment Clause . . . . It is neither sacrilegious nor antireligious to say that each separate government in this country should stay out of the business of writing or sanctioning official prayers and leave that purely religious function to the people themselves and to those the people choose to look to for religious guidance."

The Engel case dealt with a prayer, however innocuous, prepared and sponsored by governmental authority. One year later, however, on June 17, 1963, the Supreme Court rendered an even more far-reaching decision. The Court held, 8-1, that Pennsylvania's Bible-reading statute and Baltimore's rule requiring the recitation of the Lord's Prayer or the reading of the Bible at the opening of the public school day were unconstitutional under the Establishment Clause of the First Amendment. In neither case was attendance at the school exercises compulsory. Justice Clark concluded for the majority as follows:

"The place of religion in our society is an exalted one, achieved through a long tradition of reliance on the home, the church and the inviolable citadel of the individual heart and mind. We have come to recognize through bitter experience that it is not within the power of government to invade that citadel . . . In the relationship between man and religion, the state is firmly committed to a position of neutrality."

So divided has been the reaction of the public, the leaders of the faiths and opinion moulders that constitutional amendments have been introduced, designed to overturn the Supreme Court decision. The first of these was the Becker Amendment in 1963, the text of which follows:

Section 1. Nothing in this Constitution shall be deemed to prohibit the offering, reading from, or listening to prayers or biblical scriptures, if participation therein is on a voluntary basis, in any governmental or public school, institution or place.

5

Section 2. Nothing in this Constitution shall be deemed to prohibit making reference to, belief in, reliance upon, or invoking the aid of, God or a Supreme Being, in any governmental or public institution or place or upon any coinage, currency, or obligation of the United States. Section 3. Nothing in this article shall constitute an establishment of religion.

Thus far, there has been no marked progress toward moving this Amendment through Congress.

The second amendment proposed was that of Senator Dirksen of Illinois (in 1966) which would authorize the providing for or permitting of "voluntary participation" in prayer but would prohibit school authorities from prescribing the "form or content" of the prayer. There has been no appreciable movement on this amendment either.

Released Time

Within four decades, all but two of the fifty states have put "released time" programs into operation. Under these programs, children are excused from school, with the consent of their parents in order to receive religious instruction. It is estimated that some 27 million public school children in about 3,000 communities are presently enrolled in these programs.

In 1948, the Supreme Court held (McCullum v. Board of Education) that such classes may not constitutionally be held on school premises. But in 1952, when confronted with the actual situation of released time classes conducted off school premises and without pressure on youngsters to participate, the Court held such practices valid under the First Amendment (Zorach v. Clauson).

The related problem of the use of school premises by religious groups at one point or another have been beneficiaries of communal sentiment in favor of opening the school doors to pressed parishes and congregations or where emergencies are involved. While issues are formulated in the legal and constitutional arena, the public generally and frequently crosses the "wall of separation."

Severe community tensions have been engendered where the issue of Christmas observance in the schools has been raised. Generally, where such observances have been traditional in preponderantly Christian communities, the objection of newer Jewish residents has touched off conflict. Thus far, however, there has been no articulate attempt to have the matter resolved legally.

The spectrum of opinion ranges from those who would perpetuate the established tradition, including the celebration of the Nativity itself. Others favor the screening of such observances to eliminate purely doctrinal aspects, including the Nativity. Still others suggest the introduction of Hanukah observance as a type of balance to the Christmas observance. At the far end of the spectrum are those who feel that religious holiday observances of any faith are outside the purview of the school and a violation of the First Amendment.

Whether the Supreme Court decisions on matters of Bible reading and prayers in the schools will lead inevitably to a test of the legality of religious holiday observations remains to be seen.

Government Aid to Education

Yet another aspect of the overall issue of religion and the schools is the degree to which government assistance may be rendered to students of parochial institutions. Opponents of such aid take the position that, in essence, this is aid to a religious or religiously-sponsored institution. Those who favor such aid point out that the benefit is for the student and his family and that the aid afforded the institution thereby is incidental. The law, as well as public opinion, is fairly split.

BUS TRANSPORTATION: In 1947, the Supreme Court decided (Everson v. Board of Education) that it was not unconstitutional for the State of New Jersey to furnish bus transportation to children in attendance at parochial schools under the same terms and conditions as such transportation was furnished to public school students. The service was characterized as a "welfare benefit" for students.

At least eight states have affirmatively held to the contrary under their state constitutions. These are: Alaska, Delaware, Maine, Missouri, New Mexico, Oklahoma, Washington and Wisconsin. Pennsylvania, in 1963, defeated a bill providing for tax-paid bus transportation in behalf of parochial school children. In Ohio, the Attorney-General ruled that no authority existed for bus transportation to be furnished to students at private and parochial schools, but indicated that legislation providing such authority would be constitutional.

States which have upheld the validity of furnishing bus transportation are: California, Connecticut, Maryland, Massachusetts and New Mexico.

TEXTBOOKS: As early as 1930 (Cochran v. Louisiana State Board of Education) the Supreme Court held that it was constitutional for the states to enact statutes providing free textbooks for children in non-public schools. Yet, only four states--Louisiana, Mississippi, Rhode Island and West Virginia--now supply textbook aid for non-public schools. Seven other states which had previously provided such aid have since invalidated it.

TUITION: Some of the states whose courts have held that the use of State funds to pay parochial school tuition is invalid are: Kentucky, Mississippi, South Dakota, Vermont and Virginia.

FEDERAL AID: In a special message to Congress in January, 1963, President John F. Kennedy offered a comprehensive plan to provide funds for education from elementary through graduate school. A bill designed to carry out this program (H. S. 3000, described as the National Improvement Act of 1963) included aids for church-related as well as public educational institutions. In higher education, particularly, church-related schools were to be made eligible for massive aid: construction loans for academic facilities; loans and grants for the construction of library facilities and for books; grants for the expansion of graduate schools, applicable to construction, faculty, and

8

equipment; increased appropriations for foreign language studies; expansion of the scope of teacher institutes, and grants to strengthen the preparation of elementary- and secondary-school teachers and teachers of gifted, handicapped, and retarded children. In addition, there were provisions for loans, work-study programs, and graduate fellowships for students in church-related colleges. Among the provisions for elementary and secondary education, the bill extended the National Defense Education Act, which provided loans to parochial and other non-public schools for science, mathematics, and foreign-language teaching equipment.

In February, 1963, the House Education and Labor Committee began hearings on the bill. It soon became clear that the higher-education features would have fairly clear sailing. In May, the administration abandoned its comprehensive aid-to-education bill in favor of separate measures, and in August the House passed a college-aid bill, which included aid to church-related colleges. It overwhelmingly rejected an amendment which would have paved the way for judicial review of the church-state aspects of the measures.

In the Senate, Winston L. Prouty (Rep., Vt.) and Wayne Morse (Dem., Ore.) clashed over the constitutionality of grants, as distinguished from loans, to church-related colleges. Prouty favored grants and loans for construction purposes, calling it "patently absurd" to question the constitutionality of aiding the construction of science classrooms in church-related colleges. Morse, on the other hand, thought the church-related college should be excluded from tax-raised grants because it exercises a religious influence over its students, but that loans would not violate the First Amendment "if the interest covers the cost of the use of the money." Sam J. Ervin (Dem., N.C.) questioned the constitutionality of both loans and grants to church-controlled colleges and universities and offered an amendment for judicial review which was included in the bill adopted by the Senate.

In November, 1963, a House-Senate conference committee reached agreement on a bill, the Senate conferees yielding on the judicial-review section. Grants were for "academic facilities," especially "designed for instruction or research in the natural or physical sciences, mathematics, modern foreign languages, or engineering, or for use as a library" and for "for sec-

9

tarian instruction or . . . religious worship." The bill provided that if its conditions for the use of facilities were met, such facilities would become the property of the private institution after a period of 20 years. It authorized an expenditure of $1.195 billion for the first three years of a five-year program and provided for a reexamination of the program before funds were authorized for the remaining two years. In November the House approved the conference committee report 258-92. In signing the measure into law in December, 1963, President Lyndon B. Johnson called it the most significant education bill in history, the first broad assistance program for colleges since the Land Grant Act a century earlier.

The New York Times applauded the "great advance" represented by the college-aid bill, but regretted the "blurring of the lines of separation of church and state. The pragmatic compromise that took final form in the bill evolved from the almost insoluble mixtures of various degrees of church-relatedness in different colleges. What matters now is that the compromise be regarded as unfortunate, if perhaps necessary, step under the special circumstances of America's peculiar higher education system--and not as a foot in the door."

The college-aid bill was followed in 1965 by the first large-scale comprehensive bill dealing with elementary and secondary school education, the Elementary and Secondary Education Act of 1965. The Act does not provide for direct grants or loans to parochial schools or their students but several of its provisions do benefit these schools and their students. Under the Act, money is made available for special educational services and arrangements for the benefit of "educationally deprived children" in private elementary and secondary schools; for the acquisition of library resources, textbooks and other teaching materials and for supplemental educational centers and services. In 1965, Congress also passed the Higher Education Act of 1965. Aid is provided for both public and private institutions. There are provisions for college library assistance, training and research, for scholarship assistance and for grants to strengthen developing institutions. The implications of the church-state issue arising from all these bills have thus far been intentionally muted.

Notwithstanding what appears to be increasing restriction by judicial fiat on the admixture of religious and secular activities, in other areas, there appears to be relatively little challenge. Thus, the tax-exempt status of religious institutions appears quite secure, and recent tax legislation has, in fact, liberalized deductions taken for contributions to such institutions. Apparently, there is a distinction as to what it is appropriate to do with the tax dollar once collected as distinguished from the basis of exempting it from collection in the first place.

Similarly, seemingly inconsistent are such widely varied practices as the impression on coins of "In God We Trust," the mention of the deity in the pledge of allegiance, provision for chaplains in the Armed Forces, clergymen in service at sessions of Congress, presidential proclamations on Thanksgiving day and a host of other evidences that there is acknowledgment of a Supreme Being. Perhaps, the test is simply that, in the schools, where the setting is one of indoctrination, the religious objective has no place.

II. OTHER FIRST AMENDMENT ISSUES

To some extent, the issue of "freedom from religion" has tended to obscure that of "freedom of religion." But since the days of Roger Williams, the country has progressed increasingly toward acceptance of the minority point of view as dictated by religious conscience.

While, in general, the law follows the prescript that "we render to Caesar the things that are Caesar's," governmental tolerance of non-conformity based in religious conviction has broadened. Thus, while in 1940 (Minersville v. Gobitis) the power of the state to require the flag salute in public schools was upheld against the assertion by a family of Jehovah's Witnesses that this ceremony was contrary to their religious belief, three years later, (West Virginia v. Barnette) the Court reversed itself and came to the opposite conclusion.

In like manner, the treatment in World War II of "conscientious objectors" was far more sympathetic than it had been in World War I. However, religious belief has not been permitted to justify polygamy. Inversely, the jurisdiction of the state over public education is not so broad or inclusive as to permit a state to render a parochial school system illegal.

A legal paradox was created in connection with the issue of the entitlement to unemployment benefits of a person whose religious convictions keep him from accepting employment requiring work on Sunday.

While the Court decided (Sherbert v. Verner) on the same day that it ruled Bible reading and the Lord's Prayer recitation invalid, that the Government had no right to impose a choice which puts a burden on the free exercise of religion, the question arises whether unemployment benefits, representing tax moneys, when paid to a person whose entitlement stems from pursuit of certain religious beliefs, is not in effect an assistance to religion. Justice Stewart, the perennial dissenter in the prayer cases, and perhaps with judicial tongue in cheek, stated the proposition:

> "If Mrs. Sherbert's refusal to work on Saturday were based on indolence, no one would argue that she was not available for work. But because her refusal . . . was based upon her religious creed, the Establishment Clause requires that she be paid unemployment compensation benefits, thus requiring financial support of government to be placed behind a particular religious belief."

Perhaps a more practical paradox is the clearcut inconsistency of this decision with the 1961 upholding of Sunday closing-laws (Braunfeld v. Brown). Both cases involved the issue of choice between livelihood and religion. Justices Harlan and White took the position that the Sherbert decision overruled Braunfeld, but they were a concurring majority only.

An analogous issue involved the vacation of conviction of one Mrs. Owen Jenison, who had been sentenced by a lower Minnesota court to 30 days in jail for refusing to take a juror's oath, which she alleged was "against her Bible." The Sherbert holding was regarded as controlling.

On the issue of closing laws, New York State has now enacted an option to the City of New York to exempt Saturday observers from the provisions of the state's Sunday closing statute. The measure was limited to family businesses only. Exercising the option, the City Council enacted an ordinance in implementation. Thus was brought to final, although only partial, fruition a long struggle to bring relief from the strictures of the state's closing law to the largest Jewish community in the world.

Freedom of Expression

In its over-all context, freedom of expression connotes the broad freedom to communicate, a concept that goes beyond mere speech. It embraces the prerogative of the free citizen to express himself, verbally or on paper, without previous restraint. If the expression meets the test of truth, the prerogative necessarily extends to the post-utterance period. It is essential to recognize at the outset that the freedom of expression extends not only to speech, but also to such areas as press, assembly, even lawful picketing and other demonstrative protests.

Censorship

Indecency, obscenity, lewdness--all are forbidden by the criminal codes of the majority of the states. The typical state law, for example, provides for fine and imprisonment of a bookseller or publisher of a book or magazine that is "obscene, indecent, impure, or manifestly tends to corrupt the morals of youth." The typical state law likewise provides for fine and imprisonment of a producer or actors of a theatrical production that is "lewd, obscene, indecent, immoral or impure."

The essential question is as to what constitutes being "lewd, obscene, indecent, immoral or impure." The Supreme Court of the United States furnished a definition in the case of Roth v. United States, decided in 1957. In upholding the conviction of the defendant bookseller, the majority opinion defined "obscene material" as that "which deals with sex in a manner appealing to 'prurient interest'," i.e. material having a tendency to excite

13

lustful thoughts. By further refinement, the material must be "prurient" to the average person, applying contemporary community standards, and must be "prurient" as a whole, rather than in isolated instances. In setting out this definition, Mr. Justice Brennan noted that "sex and obscenity are not synonymous" and that "the portrayal of sex, e.g. in art, literature and scientific works, is not itself sufficient reason to deny material the constitutional protection of freedom of speech and press."

But if the work, taken as a whole, is "patently offensive" to community tastes and "is utterly without redeeming social value", it is obscene.

In subsequent key decisions on obscenity, Ginzburg v. United States and "Memoirs of a Woman of Pleasure"v. Att'y Gen'l of Mass. (The Fanny Hill case), the Supreme Court augmented and elaborated on the Roth test by stating that each of these three overlapping criteria must be independently satisfied and added the additional standard that evidence of "pandering" or commercial exploitation in the production, sale and publicity of the material could be used to judge whether it is obscene.

Application of these tests since Roth and Ginzburg has led the Court to an ever stricter definition of what is "obscene." As one civil liberties lawyer has put it, "obscenity is a matter of geography," the attitude of communities determining the degree to which pornography will be prosecuted. As a result, as pointed out in an exhaustive article on the growth of pornography as "big business" in the New York Times of February 22, 1970, producers of such material--publishers, film makers and the like--press for Court tests, reasonably secure in the knowledge that the frontier of what is permissible and protected under the First Amendment will be increasingly expanded. Responsive to public outcries, mayors, licensing commissioners, private "decency" organizations and religious organizations undertake, from time to time, to enforce, either by law or custom, their "standards of decency." But these efforts generally run afoul of the procedural safeguards which the Court has read into the operation of censorship machinery. Combined with the changing mores which embrace a more permissive attitude toward sex, the pornographers point to their sales as indicative of increasing public acceptance of their wards. In the final analysis, we

14

appear headed toward a standard of personal and individual choice, with perhaps the attempt to protect children against exposure to pornography as the last line of legal defense.

A major redefinition of obscenity was established in 1973 when the Supreme Court's new majority repudiated the "utterly without redeeming social importance" test as too strict. In its place the Court has now supplied a new definition. The test includes three elements -- whether "the average person, applying contemporary community standards" would find that the work, taken as a whole, appeals to the prurient interest; whether the work depicts or describes in a patently offensive way, sexual conduct specifically defined by the applicable state law; and whether the work, taken as a whole, lacks serious literary, artistic, political, or scientific value. Thus the basic elements of the test have change significantly, and many works that would have been legally protected under the "hard core" test are at least vulnerable under the new standard.

In addition, the Court has changed the source of the standards to be applied in judging obscenity. Under the test of the 1960's, the standard was to be a national one, so that works which circulated freely in New York City could not be banned in communities with less liberal tastes. Now, however, the court has reintroduced the local community as the source of standards. In Miller v. California (1973), the U.S. Supreme Court held that "The adversary system, with lay jurors as the ultimate fact-finders in criminal prosecutions, has historically permitted triers-of-fact to draw on the standards of their community, guided always by limiting instructions on the law. To require a State to structure obscenity proceedings around evidence of a national community standard would be an exercise in futility."

Against this background of disintegrating censorship machinery, it is nevertheless useful to explore how it works with respect to theatrical productions, books and magazines, motion pictures, radio and TV and the mails.

Theatrical productions

The staging of an "obscene" play leaves the producer and the actors liable to criminal prosecution. The theater in which

15

such a play is housed, moreover, runs the risk of losing its license.

Frequently, actors are willing for prosecution, content in the knowledge that a jury will not convict. Producers and theater owners, however, with much more to lose in terms of financial investment, are seldom willing to risk prosecution. The mere threat of prosecution is usually sufficient to get them to take a play off the boards, the feelings of the actors notwithstanding.

This means that the real enforcement of a morality code rests not with a jury in a criminal proceeding after a play has been presented, but with an official censor who may ban it in advance of presentation. Such an official dramatic censor operates in Boston. In New York City, the licensing commissioner operates as censor, sometimes, as in the days of Mayor La Guardia, with the vigilant assistance of the mayor. In other cities, the police commissioner is the guardian of public morals.

In this scheme of things, the state laws become almost inoperative. Municipal enforcement by advance censorship becomes the rule.

Books and magazines

Plays, burlesques and other forms of entertainment have generally been regarded by the courts as not involving the issue of freedom of expression. This has been true despite the fact that it is a very thin line that separates "entertainment" from "exposition of an idea," particularly in the serious play that may deal with sex or morals in an unorthodox way.

Where books and magazines are involved, however, the issue of freedom of press is clearly posed, and advance censorship becomes doubtful. An influential publisher will frequently risk criminal prosecution, knowing that his mass volume business will not suffer too greatly if he goes to bat for a particular book. Morever, if he wins, the fact that a book has become controversial will establish it as a best seller. For the publisher, the risk of criminal prosecution may be good business.

For the bookseller, however, criminal prosecution presents the same risk encountered by the producer of an "obscene" play. Successful criminal prosecution can put so great a drain on him that he can be put out of business. Accordingly, book-sellers have sought some means of advance clearance of books in order to avoid these risks.

Out-and-out censorship of books and publications would violate freedom of press. The law may restrain sale or distribution of certain publications which fall within narrow statutory definitions, but the law may not prevent publication. Accordingly, in many communities, either the District Attorney, the police, private organizations concerned about decency, the booksellers themselves or all four collaborate to determine in advance what publications shall be "prohibited." The word, "prohibited" is used advisedly since a bookseller who violates the informal ban would leave himself wide open to criminal prosecution. There is, of course, no appeal to the courts from the decision of informal censors.

A law passed in Massachusetts, at the instigation of the book-sellers themselves, attempts to provide for official censorship, yet within the bounds of the Constitution. Instead of a criminal prosecution against a book seller, the Massachusetts law affords the alternative of a civil proceeding against the book. Since such a suit asks a court injunction against the distribution of a particular book, the suit is one in equity, and there is no trial by jury. Trial is by a judge, and the judge thereby becomes the censor. If he finds the book to be "obscene," no bookseller will distribute it, for distribution would mean criminal prosecution. It was this proceeding by which the Fanny Hill case reached the Supreme Court resulting in a finding that the book was not obscene. Section 22-a of New York City's Code of Criminal Procedure likewise provides for action for a permanent injunction to prohibit the sale of obscene material. This provision has been held constitutional by the United States Supreme Court.

While the courts will seldom upset a finding of fact that a particular publication is "obscene," they will take a long look at the constitutionality of the state statute or municipal ordinance under which a prosecution is brought. In essence, any statute which seeks to go beyond the traditional concepts of lewdness and obscenity to strike down, for example, the "sacrilegious," or "accounts of crime, lust and bloodshed," are held to be too vague to be constitutional. In like manner, a Maryland statute prohibiting the display of "crime and lust" mag-

17

azines to minors has been declared invalid; a state court ruled that the prohibition can lie only against sale.

Motion pictures

In 1915, the Supreme Court, holding that movies were strictly entertainment and not within the orbit of constitutional protection, upheld the constitutionality of movie censorship. For nearly four decades, this decision stood unchallenged. But in 1952, in a case involving the highly controversial motion picture, The Miracle, the Court decided that refusal to license the picture on the grounds that it was "sacrilegious," was a violation of the Constitution. Shortly thereafter, the Court likewise reversed bans on films that had been condemned for "immorality," "inciting to crime and violence," and "inciting to racial tension." In all these cases, the Court ruled that the standards set by the statutes were too vague to be constitutional, and indicated that only a ban on the basis of "obscenity" under a narrowly drawn statute could be sustained.

The effect of these Supreme Court actions was to bring motion pictures within the protection of the First Amendment. This has resulted during a fifteen year period in the total disintegration of censorship. The nail in the coffin was Maryland's Freedman case, under which the burden of proof that a film should not be shown must rest on the censor; final decision rests with the courts, not the censor; and the procedure must be speedy. New York, Virginia and Kansas dismantled their state censorship machinery after this decision and Maryland's machinery became virtually inoperative.

During this same period, the attempt was made to shift responsibility to municipalities, where the approach has been in terms of ordinances requiring classification of motion pictures into "suitable" or "unsuitable." Judicial treatment of these ordinances has been varied and inconsistent. In the final analysis, however, the Freedman case, with its procedural safeguards, appears to have rendered these ordinances constitutionally dubious. Moving into the breach, as much to preempt the field from the state and municipal agencies as well as to provide a measure of industry discipline, the Motion Picture Association of America has adopted a new code of self-regulation which provides for the labeling of certain films as "suggested for mature audiences." The label, not binding on theater owners, but designed as a guide to parents, is required to be carried on advertising as well as the actual movie.

In sum, it can be said that official censorship of motion pictures is at this juncture a toothless tiger, if not a ghost. An aroused public, however, reacting in certain communities to specific motion picture vehicles, is still capable of forcing a censorship issue.

Censorship on the Federal Level

Censorship on the federal level operates in three major areas: (1) radio and TV; (2) the mails; (3) import of foreign reading matter.

RADIO AND TV: The Federal Communications Commission licences the operations of radio and TV stations. Since there are many more applicants than there are frequencies, in granting or renewing a license, the FCC must make a choice between competing applicants.

In setting minimum standards for a station licensee, the FCC, in addition to its technical and operational requirements, prescribes a basic program code that may be summarized as follows:

a. Monopoly is discouraged. While a newspaper may be granted a license to operate a radio station, it will not be granted a license where where the combined radio and newspaper control would give a communication monopoly in a community.

b. Nothing obscene or indecent may be uttered over the airwaves. While the FCC has no power to censor a broadcast nor even to issue a cease and desist order, it can suspend or subsequently deny the reissue of a license.

c. On controversial issues, where a station has given radio time to one point of view, it must provide, when requested to do so, an equal amount of time to the opposing point of view. In general, the FCC favors free time to both sides in the presentation of a controversial issue.

d. A station owner may not use his station to express his own views on controversial issues. The FCC has rejected the argument that a station owner should have the same right to express his views as a newspaper publisher. The FCC points out that while newspapers are private enterprises, radio stations

19

are licensed by the public.

e. In the granting or renewal of a license, the FCC will take into consideration the record of an applicant or station operator with respect to his fairness of approach to the various ethnic and social groups within the community. Stations sponsoring or allotting program time to "hate" groups or deliberately excluding a pro-labor point of view from the air run the risk of losing their licenses, when they come up for renewal.

A decision by the U.S. Court of Appeals for the District of Columbia in a matter involving the Federal Communications Commission on an issue of racially biased programming established the right of citizens groups to complain and be heard before the agency. Said the Court, "Since the concept of standing is a functional one . . . to insure that only those with a . . . legitimate interest can participate . . . we can see no reason to exclude those with such an obvious and acute concern as the listening audience. This . . . seems essential to insure that (licensed broadcasters) be responsive to the needs of the audience."

This same case, as well as others, also involved the FCC's Fairness Doctrine, which provides that if a station airs an issue of public importance it must present other sides of the question. The FCC seeks to go even further in attempting to assure an opportunity to respond to personal attacks on radio or TV, a requirement held constitutional by the Supreme Court. The FCC proposes that a station be required to send a tape, transcript or summary of the charges to the attacked person or group no later than one week after the attack is made. In the heat of political campaigns, the FCC suggests that political candidates receive notice within 24 hours of a station's editorial opposition to them.

The combination of citizen participation at FCC hearings and the Fairness Doctrine preserve the integrity of freedom of speech, while making possible practical remedies for abuse. In passing, one must take note of Vice President Spiro Agnew's attack on the TV networks and other media for what he felt to be "slanted" reporting.

MAILS: By federal law and by post office regulations, obscene or fraudulent matter is barred from the mails, as is the use of the mails to conduct a lottery or to engage in other specified unlawful activity. In addition, matter which violates the provisions of the Federal Espionage Act is also barred.

Where the mails are being used to carry obscene publications or as a means of fraudulent representation, the Post Office may either exclude such publications totally from the mails, or where the publisher or distributor enjoys a second class mailing privilege, may revoke this privilege. In the past, where matter has been banned from the mails, there has usually been no hearing; where revocation of second class mailing privilege is involved, there has generally been a hearing before the postal authorities.

Since the attempt to mail forbidden matter is a criminal offense, post office action, at one and the same time, may ban a particular item from the mails, and by so doing, render the party that sought to mail the item criminally liable. Here, censorship does not prevent the risk of criminal prosecution, but creates it.

Up until quite recently, there was only a very narrow court review of the actions of the postal authorities. In the Esquire case, however, substantial inroads were made on Post Office censorship. The Post Office had sought to deny the second class mailing privileges of Esquire Magazine, chiefly on the grounds that it did not contain information of a public character.

The case was taken up to the Supreme Court which decided that the authority of the Post Office nowhere includes the right to revoke mailing privileges because a publication does not contain information of a public character. The revocation of Esquire mailing privileges was reversed, the Court holding that the Post Office may no longer deny second class mailing privileges because of the contents of a publication. It may, however, after hearing, declare particular issues of publications, books, or pamphlets non-mailable.

At about the same time that the Esquire case was in the courts, orders barring from the mails a publication on birth control and another on sex adjustment in marriage were reversed by federal courts. Since the Esquire decision, the Post Office has been very cautious in the exercise of its powers to ban on grounds of obscenity. In fact, several Supreme Court justices have doubted the P.O.'s power to ban as distinguished from bringing criminal proceedings. However, mail fraud orders continue to be issued wherever the postal authorities feel that the matter being mailed contains exaggerated claims. (The subject of false advertising is beyond the scope of this work.)

IMPORT OF FOREIGN READING MATTER: The Customs Bureau exercises preliminary power in screening foreign produced reading matter and films for obscenity or for advocating or urging treason, insurrection or forcible resistance to any law of the United States. However, customs inspectors do not have the final decision. Court proceedings are required to confiscate or destroy a book for obscenity or other stated reasons. Either party can demand a jury trial.

Fair Comment v. Contempt

Since the famed trial of Peter Zenger, the New York printer, for sedition in colonial times, the freedom of newspapers from restriction has been synonymous with freedom of the press. As a result, attempted censorship of newspapers has never been extensive. The major issue has revolved around devices for preventing hostile newspaper criticism of public officials.

A Minnesota law of 1925, known as the "Minnesota Gag Law," provided for injunction against malicious, scandalous, defamatory and obscene newspapers, magazines and publications. Truth was a defense only if matter was published with good motives and for justifiable ends. Injunction could be granted not only against objectionable issues of newspapers or publications but could completely stop a newspaper or publication from publishing. The Supreme Court invalidated this statute as an improper interference with freedom of the press.

The Supreme Court likewise struck down a more subtle attempt at press censorship by Huey Long in Louisiana. He sought to impose a 2% tax on the gross receipts of newspapers selling ad space and having a circulation of more than 20,000 per week. The law was aimed at the larger newspapers which were opposed to the Long administration. The Court held the law to be a violation of freedom of press as well as unlawful discrimination against the larger newspapers in Louisiana.

Contempt proceedings have been the most effective device for dealing with criticism of public officials, particularly judges.

A newspaper editor or publisher, fearful lest criticism of official action might lead to criminal prosecution, tends to be extremely cautious in handling of news and issues involving court cases.

The trend in the Supreme Court has been toward liberalized the law applicable to contempt proceedings. Unless the criticism creates a "clear and present danger" to the fair and orderly administration of justice, it cannot be punished summarily for contempt. The Supreme Court, in urging judges to be less sensitive to criticism, estimates that judges have too much stamina to yield to unseemly pressures.

Under the rules governing contempt, critical comment after a proceeding is concluded can never be punished, because there is no interference with the proceedings which can result from the criticism. As to comment made while proceedings are in progress, only comment specifically intended to influence and capable of influencing the jury, or implying a threat to the judge or jurymen, or inciting public opinion against the judge or jury with specific intent to influence their judgments may be punished.

The trial of the Chicago 7 (originally 8) for violation of the 1968 Federal Anti-riot Act has dramatized the issue of contempt. The trial judge, Julius Hoffman, after the case had gone to the jury, meted out stiff sentences to both the defendants and their attorneys on specified counts of contempt, based on conduct during the course of the trial. William Kunstler, the chief defense attorney, received a four-year sentence on several contempt counts. These sentences pose the basic question whether the summary justice involved in a judge's decision, without a jury, to commit for long prison terms on contempt charges is consistent with the Bill of Rights:

Civil and Criminal Penalties

In addition to the contempt sanction, other means exist for combatting possible abuse of freedom of the press. Money damages are available in civil suits for libel and on occasion offending press statements and commentary may run afoul of state criminal statutes. But given the exalted position of a free press in our society, attempts to restrict freedom of publication in either of these ways are closely scrutinized, particularly when the issue relates to criticism of the conduct of public affairs.

In 1964, the Supreme Court threw out a $500,000 libel judgment awarded a Montgomery, Ala., city official in a suit against the New York Times and four Negro ministers. The Court ruled that a public official may not recover damages for a defamatory falsehood relating to his official conduct without a showing of actual malice, of knowledge the statement was false or reckless disregard of whether or not it was false. Justices Black, Douglas, and Goldberg, in concurring opinions, enunciated a doctrine of unconditional freedom of the public and press to criticize official conduct.

And recently, in reversing the libel award of a New Hampshire jury in favor of a former supervisor of a county-operated recreation center, the Supreme Court made it clear that newspaper criticism of the operations of government is protected. Such comment may not be suppressed at the behest of an individual government official--this smacks of the use of personal defamation suits as a substitute for constitutionally prohibited prosecutions for "seditious libel." Mr. Justice Douglas would extend the court's formulation of the "public official" test of the New York Times case to prevent recovery of damages for any criticism related to a "public issue" and Justice Black's view is that the First Amendment bars the recovery of damages by anyone who is a "public agent" whether an official or not.

One step removed from this is the question of whether individuals who are neither elected or appointed public officials or public agents in any customary sense, but who have become prominent can recover damages for alleged libel by the press or for invasion of a right of privacy. A federal district court in Kentucky has answered no in a case involving former Army Major General Edwin Walker who the court said had become a "public man." A jury in Texas on the other hand, awarded General Walker $500,000 against the Associated Press for its reports of the same incident which involved desegregation of the University of Mississippi in 1962. In the meantime, the Supreme Court has held in Time, Inc. v. Hill that an individual whose family's real life experience had been to some extent fictionalized and dramatized in a play, could not recover damages against Life Magazine for an invasion of the right of privacy without showing that the magazine article which linked the family's experience to the play contained "knowing or reckless

24

falsity."

Attempts at punishing libel by criminal sanctions are rarely successful. In 1952, the Supreme Court sustained an Illinois criminal statute as applied to a publication which defamed a racial group, and, moreover, which was likely to foment violence. This resulted from the exceptional circumstances of that particular publication. The more normal result of criminal libel prosecutions is that of Garrison v. Louisiana decided a short time after the New York Times case in which the court held that criminal defamation statutes may not be used to prohibit comment, made without actual malice, on the conduct of public affairs.

Another issue is the extent to which criminal sanctions may be imposed to prevent the expression of views on matters that are before the electorate. In 1962, a Birmingham, Alabama, newspaper editor published an editorial on election day urging voters to adopt a new form of city government. He was prosecuted for violating a state law prohibiting electioneering on election day. The Supreme Court later held that such a prosecution violated the First Amendment's guarantee of freedom of speech and the press.

B. Police Power Regulation

As has been previously noted, freedom of expression does not cover the obscene, the fraudulent or the libelous. Such expression is regarded as not being part of the exposition of an idea, and therefore not "speech" at all, in the sense that the First Amendment to the Constitution seeks to protect.

But there is speech that is part of the exposition of an idea which may, nevertheless, be subject to regulation. What, for example, is the law when a belief is expressed that is offensive to other persons? Or, when the method of expression fails to meet certain basic requirements?

In general, the answers to these questions involve a weighing of the freedom of expression on the one hand, against the regulatory police power of the state, on the other. Through the 1940's, the Supreme Court in a series of cases dealing with the efforts of the respective states to curb the Jehovah's Witnesses, a religious sect often displaying substantial fanaticism, came close to giving full rein to freedom of expression. The freedoms guaranteed by the First Amendment were said to be "preferred liberties." More recently, this full freedom has been somewhat circumscribed by the Court, and the right of the state to regulate in behalf of the welfare of its people has come to be entitled to equal consideration. (See infra p.25, "Law and Order") The rules, as they emerge from a welter of somewhat confusing opinions, may be summarized as follows:

Prior Restraints; Licensing

If Mr. X expresses his religious views on a street corner, he cannot be prevented from doing so either by the police or by municipal ordinance. This is equally true for the streets of a privately owned company town. If he were to distribute handbills on the streets, or ring doorbells soliciting funds for his religious cause, he could not be forbidden to do so. Moreover, he cannot be required to seek a permit to distribute handbills. Nor can he be made to pay a license fee or tax to sell pamphlets of a religious nature on the streets or by door-to-door canvass. If, however, he is a commercial magazine peddler, his door-to-door canvassing can be regulated.

Mr. X can be required to register with the police for purposes of identification if he desires to solicit funds. This is regarded as a means of protecting the community against possible fraud. But he cannot be required to salute the flag as a condition of his distributing literature or soliciting funds.

If Mr. X desires to organize a religious parade through the streets of his city, he can be required to obtain a license, so long as the licensing official has no discretion to censor the purpose of the parade, but only the authority to weigh considerations like traffic, public safety, etc. In like manner an open-air park meeting can be licensed, but not on the basis of content of the speeches. The obstruction of public passageways and thoroughfares can be forbidden by law enforcement authorities, and likewise, the authorities can determine the appropriate uses for parks and recreational facilities. What is forbidden the licensing authority is the right to discriminate between one cause and another in terms of granting a license.

If, in the course of a private discussion, Mr. X makes offensive references to religions other than his own, there is no question of his right to express his opinions. But if he were to come uninvited into a hotel or privately owned establishment insisting on making his opinions known to unwilling listeners, he could be convicted of disorderly conduct. Freedom of expression does not include the right to interfere with another's enjoyment of his property.

But if he makes the same remarks at a public meeting place, he can be successfully prosecuted only if his remarks incite to riot or to a breach of the peace. Moreover, he is legally accountable only for a breach of the peace that results from his own incitation, but not for a breach of the peace that is occasioned by the reactions of his antagonists.

The mere possibility of disturbance is not enough; to warrant prosecution, the breach must be imminent or actual. In the absence of such clearcut breach of the peace, prosecution and conviction are possible only under a statute narrowly drawn to define and punish specific conduct as constituting a clear and present danger to a substantial interest of the state. Some states, particularly sensitive to attacks against racial, religious, and ethnic groups, have adopted such specific, narrowly drawn statutes. "Race Hate" laws seek to punish the incitement to or advocacy of hatred against particular ethnic or religious groups in the community. "Group Libel" laws empower the Attorney-General of a state to prosecute those who, with malicious intent to promote hatred, issue false written or printed material about particular ethnic, racial, or religious groups in the community. State laws of one or the other type described exist in Illinois, Indiana, Massachusetts, New Mexico, and New Jersey, but they are seldom invoked. The New Jersey law was declared unconstitutional in 1942 for being too vague and indefinite.

The First Amendment, however, does not protect profane or abusive language. If Mr. X, on being accosted by a police officer, uses abusive and profane language, he can be prosecuted for disorderly conduct. In like manner, the First Amendment protects normal speech, but may not protect speech that

27

is amplified by a loud-speaker or sound-truck apparatus. The Supreme Court has made clear that regulations as to time, place and volume of sound are constitutional, and has even intimated that, although a municipality may not license sound trucks, they may be banned altogether.

If Mr. X. in expressing his religious opinions, advocates the doing of something that is against the law, he may be prosecuted and convicted. But the law under which he is prosecuted must be specific and definite. The Supreme Court reversed the conviction of a group of Mormons who had advocated polygamy in one of their publications, and the case was remanded to Utah courts to consider whether the law under which they had been prosecuted was "vague and indefinite."

Where a valid licensing procedure exists, Mr. X. cannot take the law into his own hands by arranging for a parade without a license after he had been denied a license. The Supreme Court has held that the aggrieved party must seek court assistance in ordering the issuance of a license, but cannot proceed without a license.

But does this rule apply in all circumstances? Since a licensing procedure which permits a licensing official to discriminate on prohibited grounds such as race or religion is not valid, there is a substantial question whether the person discriminated against must apply for a license or can proceed without one. This issue arose in Birmingham, Alabama, in 1963 during racial demonstrations there when city officials consistently refused to grant Negroes seeking such things as the right of access to public places, non-discriminatory hiring and courtesy treatment from merchants, a permit to hold demonstrations. Nevertheless, demonstrations occurred and several arrests were made. The Supreme Court has now decided that the Negro demonstrators were acting within their rights in deciding to press their demonstrations in the face of this official conduct.

Peddlers of Ideas

What emerges from the foregoing is that the "peddler of ideas" is generally free from prior restraint that smacks of censorhip of his views. Taxes, discretionary licensing arrangements and discriminatory administrative regulations are invalid. However, considerations of public welfare, use of public property, traffic control and similar factors, consistently applied, can furnish the basis for a valid licensing system. In general, speech itself is freer than the availability of public places for it. Convictions for breach of the peace or disorderly conduct will be sustained only if it can be affirmatively shown that an actual or imminent breach of the peace occurred and that it was directly caused by the advocacy of the defendant. Moreover, to be actionable, the threat of violence must be created by the speaker, not by the possible reactions of a hostile crowd.

In recent years, as protests, picketing and demonstrations have multiplied in connection with the expression of points of view on such major issues as the Viet Nam War, black militancy, campus revolt, and similar issues on which heated passions have a built-in potential for violence, the Supreme Court (through the tenure of Chief Justice Warren) has held to the line of the earlier cases. Thus in Gregory v. City of Chicago, involving the disorderly conduct conviction of Dick Gregory, the Court reversed the conviction holding that the First Amendment protects peaceful and orderly protest marchers. In Shuttlesworth v. City of Birmingham (Alabama), the Court reversed convictions for violating a city ordinance requiring a parade permit; and an order restraining rallies or meetings by a racist organization was held invalid in Joseph Carroll v. President and Commissioners of Princess Anne. A school regulation prohibiting students from wearing black armbands as a protest against the Viet Nam War was held to violate the right to free speech in Tinker v. Des Moines Independent Community School District.

C. Law and Order

These same issues are at the root of the socio-legal phenomenon of "law and order," a coverall phrase for invoking the power of the government to repress militant protest.

Actually an extension of police power regulation, "law and order" is here treated separately because it involves, in addition to renewed attempts of the states to regulate alleged antisocial conduct, the entry of the federal government into areas normally comprised by the police power of the states. While the federal government has traditionally legislated in areas affecting national security, (see infra, PROTECTION OF NATIONAL SECURITY) it has generally left to the states the matter of seeking to define the point at which certain conduct becomes no longer free expression but a violation of law. (As appears from the prior section on Police Power Regulation, the Supreme Court has often struck down the efforts of the states to enact or enforce these definitions on the grounds that they are too vague or too indefinite or actually impose illegal limits on freedom of expression.)

The Federal Anti-Riot Act of 1968 (actually a rider to the 1968 Civil Rights Act), which was used to bring to trial the Chicago 7 for conspiracy and incitement to riot at the Democratic Convention in Chicago in 1968 and the Omnibus Crime Control and Safe Streets Act of 1968 are clearcut examples of federal legislation in areas ordinarily cognizable in state courts. The rationale is based partially on the protection of the national security and partially on the premise that incitement to violence is frequently an organized effort which crosses state lines, and is therefore a federal problem properly dealt with by the federal government. Undoubtedly, the Chicago 7 case will provide the basis for ultimate determination by the Supreme Court of the constitutionality of the Anti-Riot Act. There would appear to be little chance of successfully challenging the Act on the grounds of invasion of the police power reserved to the states. The federal attorneys can clearly make out a case for the federal government's right to legislate against violence across state lines. The essential question therefore remains whether the legislation illegally punishes freedom of speech and assembly, or validly punishes the abuses of those freedoms. Specifically, is there a right to be a peaceful outside agitator, or is this conduct which Congress has a right to proscribe? In November, 1969, for example, it was announced that the FBI would investigate whether leaders of the peaceful November Moratorium (Viet Nam) in Washington had violated the Anti-Riot Act.

It remains to be seen whether the changing make-up of the Supreme Court under Chief Justice Warren Burger will result in a less permissive approach to these First Amendment issues than the Roosevelt, Vinson and Warren courts which, case by case, over the last 30 years, have hammered out the law in this area.

The Nixon Administration, particularly as reflected through the office of Attorney-General Mitchell and the Department of Justice, as well as the public utterances of Vice President Agnew, has made it clear that the pursuit of "law and order" is a major Administration policy. Those critical of this policy have likened the current trend to the period of repression identified with Attorney-General Palmer in the Harding Administration. The Administration, on the other hand, asserting its representation of the "silent majority," interprets its policies in terms of tempering the traditional scope for freedom of expression by protection for the majority of the citizenry against the tyranny of militant minorities. In general it can be said that the Administration's tone has encouraged local law enforcement officers to crack down on dissent.

II. PROTECTION OF NATIONAL SECURITY

How far is a free and democratic society obliged to extend its freedom to individuals or organizations dedicated to the over-throw of its form of government? In weighing individual freedom against the requirements of national security, courts and legis-latures alike have been faced with the most penetrating problem of our times.

The government has never been powerless to deal with crimes of action against the state. There have always been adequate laws on the books against treason, sabotage, espionage, and var-ious activities designed to weaken our military or industrial es-tablishments. These laws generally do not involve a conflict be-tween individual freedom and national security.

It is at the point that the government seeks to define and pun-ish crimes of advocacy that the issue of freedom of expression of the individual is drawn. As to when advocacy may be punished, the tests laid down by the Supreme Court have differed from pe-riod to period, generally depending on the state of the nation and the shape of world affairs at a given time.

In the aftermath of World War I, for example, when the gov-ernment rode herd on anarchists, syndicalists and a variety of political radicals, advocacy of a point of view could be punished if it exhibited a "dangerous tendency." The vast network of state laws outlawing red flags, and seeking to punish anarchists, syn-dicalists and the exponents of similar political ideas were gener-ally sustained on the grounds that such advocacy created a dan-gerous tendency in the direction of bringing about what was being advocated by the spokesman. It made no difference under this test whether what was being advocated could in fact be feasibly brought about.

During the thirties, the Court took another look at political radicalism, and found it to be much less of a threat to the na-tional security. Accordingly, what had been the minority point of view as expounded by such jurists as Holmes and Brandeis, emerged as the majority opinion, and the Court held that for advocacy to be punished, it had to create a "clear and present danger" of bringing about the very evil with which the state had the right to deal. Just as the dangerous tendency test almost inevitably led to sustaining conviction, the clear and present danger test almost inevitably led to reversing conviction. Under this test, for example, a Communist preaching the overthrow of the government could not be punished for his utterances unless there was a clear and present danger demonstrated that his utterances would lead to action.

During the forties, a reaction began to set in against the "pure" doctrine of the clear and present danger test. The feeling grew, as expressed in a variety of federal legislation, that mature political philosophies such as fascism and communism posed a threat to the national security of this country, so severe that it was not feasible to await a clear and present danger before advocacy could be restrained. The Court grappled with this problem although a number of situations, finally emerging in the Dennis case (the trial of the eleven top Communists under the Smith Act) with a new test--clear and probable danger--a sort of middle ground between dangerous tendency and clear and present danger. Although the language used by the court in the Dennis case is actually the language of the clear and present danger test, the meaning of the decision is that the government has the right to restrain advocacy when what is advocated creates an indicated likelihood that some action will be taken to bring it about. Students of civil liberties have treated this decision as establishing a test of clear and probable danger.

Against this background, it is possible to study the security machinery of the federal and state governments and the impact of this machinery on the status of civil liberty.

A. Sedition and Subversion

The first piece of sedition legislation was the Alien and Sedition acts of 1798, which authorized the President to deport aliens whom he judged to be dangerous to the peace and safety of the country, and sought to punish false and scandalous writings against the government or any of its arms, if published with intent to defame or to excite hatred. These measures were enacted at a time when the country was not actually at war. History records that they aroused powerful popular indignation which all but destroyed the Federalist Party. With the advent of Thomas Jefferson to the presidency, those imprisoned under the Sedition Law were pardoned and all fines collected were eventually repaid.

In our time, the first important sedition act was the Espionage Act of 1917, passed after our entry into the First World War. During the twenties, the pattern of prosecution for sedition in wartime was carried over to peacetime through the anarchy, syndicalism and sedition laws of the states, mentioned above. Then, in 1940, a federal peacetime sedition law was passed for the first time since 1798. This was contained in the Alien Registration Act of 1940, sometimes called the Smith Act. Analysis of both the Espionage Act of 1917 and the Smith Act will help the reader to understand the security machinery and the civil liberties considerations as well.

War Measures

The Espionage Act of 1917, which is still on the books and was applied in the Second World War as well as the First, defines three wartime offenses: (1) the willful utterance of false statement with intent to interfere with the operation or success of the armed forces of the United States; (2) the willful causing of or attempt to cause insubordination, disloyalty, mutiny or refusal of duty in the armed forces of the United States; (3) the willful obstruction of the recruiting or enlistment service of the United States. Penalties or fine of not more than $10,000 or imprisonment for not more than twenty years or both are provided. (An Amendment to this Act, passed in 1918, added nine additional offenses. The Amendment was repealed in 1921.)

The enforcement of these provisions of the Espionage Act differed widely in the two world wars. In the First World War, there were hundreds of prosecutions of persons who raised their voices against the draft and against the war. Many publications were banned from the mails and their second class mailing privileges revoked for similar utterances. In general, the courts took the position that an utterance did not have to create a "clear and present danger" to the war effort; it was sufficient if the utterance created a "dangerous tendency." Moreover, willful intent was presumed from the speech or writing. Under these tests, conviction followed almost inevitably on prosecution.

In the Second World War, there were relatively few prosecutions under the Espionage Act. Generally, they were limited to prosecutions of members of certain Negro sects for consipring to obstruct the operations of selective service, to members of the German-American Bund and to organizations and members of organizations professionally anti-Semitic, anti-government and pro-Axis.

The government and the courts took action only where there was actual incitement to violation of the law or where there was a "clear and present danger" that the illegal action urged would be taken. The Supreme Court, in the two Espionage cases which it reviewed, reversed convictions--in one case, of 28 German-American Bund leaders who had advised their members to resist certain provisions of the 1940 Draft Act which were alleged to discriminate against Bund members--in the second case, of a Chicago pamphleteer who had prepared and distributed mimeographed circulars which discouraged recruiting and enlistment. This latter case most certainly would have been decided the other way in World War I, indicating that the government gave much greater latitude to freedom of expression in the Second World War than in the First.

The Federal Peacetime Sedition Act

The Alien Registration Act of 1940 (Smith Act), to a greater extent than the Espionage Act, posed the major issues involving sedition in the Second World War. As observed previously, this law was the first peacetime Sedition Law to be enacted by Congress since 1798.

Section 1 of the Act makes the Espionage Act applicable in peacetime. Section 2 enumerates the following offenses: (1) willfully advocating the overthrow of government in the United States by force or violence; (2) willfully issuing any written or printed matter so advocating; (3) to organize any society, group or assembly of persons who so advocate; (4) to become a member of or affiliate with any such society, group or assembly, knowing its purposes. Section 3 makes it unlawful to attempt or conspire to commit the prohibited acts. The penalty is fine up to $10,000, imprisonment up to 10 years, or both.

The most significant wartime case involving the Sedition Act was the prosecution for seditious conspiracy brought in the federal court of the District of Columbia against some 29 leaders of alleged pro-Nazi movements. (This is not the Bund prosecution, mentioned above.) The action was begun in 1942 under both the Sedition Act and the Espionage Act. The court threw out the "Sedition" indictment on the grounds that the Sedition Act could not punish condict prior to 1940. The "Espionage" charges were dropped because the government was unable to uncover evidence of illegal activities after this country had gone to war.

In 1944, new indictments were brought, charging conspiracy on behalf of the German government to undermine the morale of the armed forces. Upon the death of the presiding judge in 1945, prosecution was not resumed and the proceeding lapsed.

A case only slightly less celebrated was the prosecution of the Socialist Workers Party (Trotskyites) and the CIO Teamster's union in Minneapolis on the charge that they advocated the overthrow of the government by force and violence. The prosecution rested its case on writings advocating the overthrow of the government contained in Party publications. A Workers Defense Guard, created to protect union property against destruction, was charged with being the organized means through which the attempt to overthrow the government was to be made. Although this second charge was subsequently dismissed, convictions of 18 of the persons prosecuted were secured.

Notwithstanding the fact that the case posed the issue of the constitutionality of the first federal peacetime sedition act since 1798, the Supreme Court refused to review the convictions. The lower courts rejected the argument that the prosecution should be dismissed because there was no "clear and present danger" of overthrow of the government by this group. They held that the federal statute, by specifically making it a crime to advocate overthrow of the government by force and violence, had rendered the existence of a "clear and present danger" immaterial.

The case of Dennis v. United States (341 U.S. 494, 1951) provided an answer to the constitutionality of the Smith Act. The case involved the legality of the convictions of eleven top

Communists for conspiracy to advocate the overthrow of the government under the Smith Act. It should be noted that the crime charged was conspiracy and that the element of the crime was not the overthrow of the government or even action in that direction, but only advocacy of such overthrow. In upholding the convictions, the Supreme Court upheld the constitutionality of the Smith Act, took judicial note of the menace of Communist subversive machinery, and as noted above, (see p.21) revised the test as to when advocacy may be punished:

"In each case, courts must ask whether the gravity of the evil, discounted by its improbability, justifies such invasion of free speech as is necessary to avoid the danger."

In 1957, the Court subtly modified its decision in the Dennis case. In a case involving the conviction of a group of California Communist Party leaders, a distinction was drawn between "advocacy of forcible overthrow as mere abstract doctrine" and "advocacy which incites to illegal action." In reversing the convictions, the Court held that the judge's charge to the jury in the lower court had been erroneous. Five of the defendants were freed and nine others were ordered retried.

Yet, in the Scales case (1961), the Court upheld the constitutionality of the membership clause of the Smith Act making it a crime knowingly to belong to a party that advocates the forcible overthrow of the government.

State Sedition Laws

Prior to World War I, most of the states of the union contented themselves with statutes specifying the common law offenses of "riot," "unlawful assembly," "breach of the peace," and "disorderly conduct." The common denominator of each of these offenses is conduct of an individual or group which threatens an immediate disturbance of the public peace or an immediate violation of the rights of others. In other words, conduct which creates a clear and present danger of an evil which the state has the power to regulate.

With the coming of World War I, however, the states turned increasingly to law which would punish utterances as well as acts. During the First World War, many of the states supplemented federal legislation with espionage acts of their own, often substantially more stringent. A Minnesota statute, for example, made it unlawful to say that men should not enlist in the armed forces of the United States or that residents of Minnesota should not aid in carrying on war with our enemies.

Similar laws were passed in Florida, Iowa, Louisiana, Missouri, Montana, Nebraska, New Hampshire, New Jersey, Pennsylvania, Texas, West Virginia, and Wisconsin.

In the aftermath of World War I, the increasing hostility to Radicals reinforced this mood and led to the passage of a rash of state sedition laws, designed to limit the freedom of expression of these groups in peacetime. The statutes include: (1) red flag laws; (2) criminal anarchy, syndicalism and sedition laws; (3) laws directed against Communists and the Communist Party.

In a previous edition of this volume, substantial attention was given to an analysis of each of these types of state laws which, in one form or another, exist in every state of the union. But in April, 1956, the Supreme Court in a 6-3 decision in Pennsylvania v. Nelson held that Federal legislation has pre-empted the area of prosecution for sedition. The highest court made clear that the Nelson case concerned only sedition against the United States, and that the dominant interest of the federal government precludes state intervention, and that administration of state acts would conflict with federal operations.

The reaction to the Supreme Court decision on the part of the attorney generals of the states was strongly critical, and legislation was introduced in Congress to revalidate the state sedition laws. The legislation, however, never reached the floor of either house. More recently, the states have sought to give new meaning to their sedition laws by instituting suits alleging sedition against the state, as distinguished from the nation. It seems clear, however, that this legislation has been rendered archaic and largely ineffective by the Court's action.

And yet, it may be helpful to summarize what can and cannot be done under state sedition laws:

. . . It is clearly constitutional to punish the open and direct advocacy of assassination, sabotage, destruction of property and other violent and unlawful conduct.

. . . It is probably not constitutional to convict a person under a sedition law for nothing more than membership in an organization which, as part of its program, advocates violent action. There should be some evidence of affirmative personal support for violent action to warrant conviction.

. . . It is probably not constitutional to convict a person under a sedition law for possessing and distributing literature of an organization which as part of its program advocates violent action, where the literature involved does not itself advocate either violence or unlawful acts.

. . . It is probably not constitutional to convict for peaceable advocacy of remote objectives, presently illegal.

Disclosure Requirements for Subversives

Several pieces of federal legislation are aimed at compelling disclosure of subversive agents and activities. The Foreign Agents' Registration Act of 1938, amended in 1953, requires the agents of any "foreign principal" to register with the Department of Justice, to file statements about their activities and affairs, and to identify any "political propaganda" they circulate.

The Alien Registration Act of 1940 (Smith Act), supplemented by the Immigration and Nationality Act of 1952 (see below, p. 26) requires all resident aliens in this country to be "registered" and fingerprinted and requires comprehensive information about them.

The Subversive Activities Control Act of 1950 (Title I of the Internal Security Act of 1950) requires the registration of "Communist action" (notably, the Communist Party) or "Communist-front" organizations. The procedures set out for achieving such registrations are quite complex, and no organization has registered up to this point. Under the Communist Control Act of 1954, "Communist-infiltrated" organizations were added to the two groups required to register under the 1950 Act. The constitutionality of the registration requirement of the Act with respect to the Communist Party was sustained by the Supreme Court in 1961.

However, the Act's requirement that individual members of Communist organizations register with the Attorney General raises a constitutional issue which requires--and has received-- a different resolution. The registration provisions of the Act

39

as applied to organizations are intended to limit the effectiveness of such organizations by forcing public disclosure of their nature and activities which are deemed clandestine and meretricious. But when the individual rather than the organization is ordered to register, the Fifth Amendment's ban against compulsory self-incrimination is violated and the Supreme Court so held in the Albertson case in 1965. Since individual registration requires admission of membership in the Communist Party or other communist organization, and such membership is an element of a crime under both the Subversive Activities Control Act and the membership clause of the Smith Act (See p. 23 supra.), individuals ordered to register may refuse and claim the privilege. The Court of Appeals for the District of Columbia has ruled since that the Communist Party also cannot be required to register where such registration requires disclosure of its membership lists. Moreover, as the Court made clear in Albertson, individuals need not risk prosecution for failure to register--with the heavy penalties that this entails--but may claim the privilege upon being ordered to register.

On the state level, disclosure requirements have been used by some states in an effort to maintain racial segregation. Several southern states have sought to ban the National Association for the Advancement of Colored People and to require disclosure of its membership lists. The Supreme Court ruled in 1958, in setting aside a $100,000 fine for contempt levied against the NAACP by the State of Alabama, that compulsory disclosure of membership lists is unconstitutional. In Bates v. Little Rock (1960), the Supreme Court upheld a lower court ruling voiding Arkansas laws which compel organizations to disclose membership and finances, and permit examination of records without a warrant. In the same year, the Court also invalidated another Arkansas law requiring teachers to disclose their organizational affiliations, primarily because the law was designed to expose teachers who belonged to the NAACP. Subsequently, in 1963 in the Gibson case and in 1965 in Dombrowski v. Pfister, the Court invalidated efforts by Florida and Louisiana respectively to curb organizations fostering civil rights for Negroes by attachment of the Communist brand. In these cases, the Court distinguished bona fide efforts to regulate communist activity from disingenuous attempts to stifle free expression and association.

40

In addition to its disclosure provisions, Section 6 of the Subversive Activities Control Act made it unlawful for a member of a communist organization as defined in the Act, to apply for, seek renewal of, use, or attempt to use a passport required for travel abroad. In pursuance of this section, the passports of the chairman of the American Communist Party and the editor of its theoretical organ, Political Affairs, were revoked in January, 1962. They brought suit in a federal district court seeking to overturn this administrative decision and reclaim their passports. The district court upheld the State Department's determination, but in June, 1964, when the case reached the U.S. Supreme Court, the Court, in a 6-3 decision, ruled this section of the Act unconstitutional. Justice Black, as he did in the earlier case involving the Act's registration provisions, clung to his view that the entire Subversive Activities Control Act is unconstitutional.

Aside from the question of passport denial on the ground of subversive taint--a question apparently decided by the Court's decision in the Aptheker case--what of the broader question of the authority of the executive branch of the government to impose what are thought to be reasonable restrictions on travel because of foreign policy considerations affecting all citizens? The result in the Aptheker case (under the Subversive Activities Control Act) was fairly predictable because several years earlier, the Supreme Court had ruled in Kent v. Dulles that a citizen could not be denied a passport because of his political beliefs or associations. But in Zemel v. Rusk in 1965, the Court upheld the Secretary's right to impose area restrictions which operate generally by sustaining his refusal to validate a passport for travel to Cuba. However, even though the Secretary may exercise such authority, criminal penalties may not be imposed on anyone bearing a valid passport which has not been specifically validated for travel to Cuba (United States v. Laub, decided in 1967). In other words, violation of an area restriction is not a ground for criminal prosecution; at most, the penalty will be that of revocation of the passport.

The general line of demarcation seems clear: the government cannot impinge on the right to travel abroad because it doesn't like the individual or his views, but it can establish restrictions in advance based on considerations of national policy.

Use of the mails for communist propaganda

Another national security issue involving possible subversion is the use of the mails for dissemination of communist propaganda. This issue--like the others--is a result of the existence of the First Amendment's guarantee of free speech. In Lamont v. Postmaster General in 1965, the Supreme Court resolved the issue by holding a section of the Postal Service and Federal Employees Salary Act of 1962 unconstitutional as applied to prevent the Postmaster General of the United States from delivering nonsealed mail or printed matter originating in a foreign country and containing "communist political propaganda" to an addressee in the United States without a specific request for delivery from the addressee. The Act was declared an abridgement of "the unfettered exercise of the addressee's First Amendment rights" to receive publications. The Court quoted with approval from Mr. Justice Holmes' dissenting opinion in an earlier case: "The United States may give up the Post Office when it sees fit, but while it carries it on the use of the mails is almost as much a part of free speech as the right to use our tongues."

Alien Subversion

The policy of excluding aliens believed to be subversive dates from 1903, when we began barring anarchists. Deportation of undesirable aliens, however, goes back as far as 1798 and the Alien and Sedition Acts. Under the Internal Security Act of 1950, Communists and other totalitarians were specifically denied entry into this country, and under the Immigration and Nationality Act of 1952 (Walter-McCarran Act), the provisions were made even more stringent. Under this Act, an alien may be barred from entry if any consular officials or the Attorney General knows or has reasonable grounds to believe that he will engage in activities contrary to the public security.

The 1952 Act also bars from naturalization Communists, members of Communist or Communist-front organizations, and all persons who teach, advocate, or publish the violent overthrow of the government. The ban is retroactive on those who within ten years of the application for naturalization have belonged in one of these classes. In addition, the 1952 Act sets out new grounds for denaturalization--concealing at the time of naturalization that one was a member of a subversive organization; refusing, within ten years following naturalization, to testify before a congressional committee with regard to subversive activities if the person has been convicted of contempt because of such refusal; becoming, within five years after naturalization, a member of an organization where such membership in the first place would have prevented naturalization.

Finally, the 1952 Act adds a provision permitting the deportation of any alien who is, or who at any time after his entry into the country has been a member of the various organizations designated as subversive. But the Supreme Court, in construing the membership provisions of the Act, has placed the ultimate burden in cases involving deportation of aliens for membership in the Communist Party on the government. In order to support an order of deportation, the evidence must show that the alien either was aware that he was joining the Communist Party and understood its nature, or that he had a "meaningful association" with the Party; evidence that an alien merely paid dues or attended meetings of a Party unit will not suffice. Indeed, the latest decision of the Supreme Court indicates that in all deportation proceedings, whether or not on the ground of alleged subversive activity or connection, the government must "establish the facts supporting deportability by clear, unequivocal and convincing evidence."

B. Loyalty and Security

LOYALTY-SECURITY PROGRAMS: The background of investigations into loyalty of government employees dates from 1939 when Congress passed the Hatch Act, among other things, making it unlawful for any government employee to have "membership in any political party or organization which advocates the over-throw of our constitutional form of government in the United States ." This was followed in 1941 by a Congressional appropriation to the FBI to inquire into subversive activities among government em-ployees and by the attachment of riders to appropriations bills forbidding payment to persons who advocated or were members of organizations advocating the overthrow of the government of the United States. As applied to cut off the salaries of several federal employees during the war, these riders were declared unconstitutional as bills of attainder. (A bill of attainder is one by which a legislature finds a person guilty of an offense and seeks to punish him for it without court trial.)

During the war, a start toward a comprehensive loyalty check for executive employees was undertaken. This reached a climax in 1946 when President Truman promulgated his Loyalty Order requiring investigation of all employees in the executive branch and of all persons seeking employment.

On its first promulgation, the program called for denying fed-eral employment when "on all the evidence, reasonable grounds exist for the belief that the person involved is disloyal to the gov-ernment of the United States." In 1951 the President altered the Order to bar persons about whose loyalty there was "reasonable doubt." In order to establish criteria by which disloyalty could be measured, the Order required the compiling by the Attorney General of a list of subversive organizations. Originally, this list was developed without any hearings and without any opportun-ity on the part of listed organizations to dispute the claim of being subversive. In 1951, however, the Supreme Court decided that for the Attorney General to place organizations on a subver-sive list without giving them a hearing was not permissible.

In 1953, President Eisenhower revised the "Loyalty" pro-gram of the Truman Administration. The Eisenhower "Security" program was designed to eliminate government employees who were security risks, although not necessarily disloyal. And, by seeking to reenforce the distinction between disloyalty and se-curity risk, the program sought to take some of the onus off be-ing fired from a federal job.

The Eisenhower program set up as the basic test of employee fitness a finding that "retention in employment in the federal ser-vice of the person being investigated is clearly consistent with the interests of national security." In the administration of this program, departmental loyalty boards and security officers are not limited to the use of the Attorney General's list. In 1956, the Supreme Court placed limitations on the administration of the Security program by ruling, in a 6-3 decision, that federal employees can be dismissed as security risks only if they hold sensitive jobs. The Court further held that President Eisenhower erred in 1953, when by executive order, he had extended security regulations to cover all government workers.

For the most part, the states do not have elaborate loyalty-security programs for the screening of state employees. Public school teachers constitute a notable exception, although even here permanent machinery does not exist in most states. New York State has a Security Risk Law, which authorizes the Civil Service Commission to screen all applicants for state jobs. A portion of this law and a provision of the Education Law specifically relating to teachers were held unconstitutionally vague earlier this year.

On the whole, however, the states use other techniques. In some, members of the Communist Party are kept off the election ballot by law. These include Arkansas, California, Delaware, Illinois, Indiana, Ohio, Pennsylvania, Tennessee and Wisconsin. In others, public officers and employees are screened by requiring them to take a loyalty oath. The Ober Law in Maryland and the Broyles Law in Illinois are typical.

In addition to federal and state loyalty programs, since part of the government's defense work is done under contract by private industry, security screening is required by executive order of those employed by private industry in carrying on classified projects or contracts. In addition, security programs have been developed by some private industries on their own initiative, even though they may not be engaged in defense work. As to organized labor, in addition to the loyalty oath provisions in the Taft-Hartley Act, the Communist Control Act of 1954 has provisions for identifying "Communist-infiltrated organizations," and if a labor union is found to be infiltrated it forfeits its privileges of collective bargaining. The Landrum-Griffin law contained a provision making it a crime for a communist to be a union officer or employee but this was held to be a bill of attainder by the Supreme Court in 1965.

Chapter II

GUARANTEES OF PERSONAL LIBERTY

The essence of democracy is not only the right to freedom of expression, but also the knowledge that one's personal liberty cannot be disturbed except by due process of law." Accordingly, the founding fathers wrote into the Articles of the Constitution and into the Bill of Rights a basic code of justice, protecting the individual against arbitrary action by government.

These guarantees of personal liberty include: (1) the privilege of the writ of habeas corpus (Article I, section 9); (2) protection against unreasonable searches and seizures (Fourth Amendment); (3) freedom from prosecution for serious crimes except by indictment or presentment by grand jury (Fifth Amendment); (4) the right to trial by jury in all criminal cases (Sixth Amendment); (5) the right to assistance of counsel (Sixth Amendment); (6) the right not to be a witness against oneself (Fifth Amendment); (7) the right to a fair trial consistent with due process of law (Fifth Amendment); (8) freedom from double jeopardy, i.e. no more than one criminal prosecution for the same offense (Sixth Amendment); (9) protection against excessive bail and fines and against cruel and unusual punishment (Eighth Amendment).

We have seen that the guarantees of the First Amendment, protecting freedom of expression against action by the federal government, apply equally and totally to the states by force of the Fourteenth Amendment. This is now practically true of the guarantees of personal liberty also, since increasingly, Supreme Court decisions in recent years have made more and more of these liberties effective against the states.

It is still true, however that several provisions of the Bill of Rights do not expressly bind the states. For example, the provisions of the Fifth Amendment requiring criminal prosecution to be instituted by indictment or presentment by a grand jury is a constitutional requirement in federal courts only. A state prosecution instituted by information--where the District Attorney or the Attorney General, rather than a grand jury, makes the accusation--is valid. Likewise, many of the states dispense with jury trial in minor criminal cases, and the right to counsel in criminal cases notwithstanding Gideon v. Wainwright (see below, p.57), is more extensive in federal courts than in state courts. But the major guarantees of the Bill of Rights now apply to the states. Consideration of some specific guarantees of personal liberty follows.

Habeas Corpus--Article I. Section 9

"The Constitution of the United States originally contained no bill of rights. It did, however, protect civil liberty by a few scattered clauses. Five of these clauses listed things which the new federal government might not do. It could not, save in times of rebellion or acute public danger, suspend the writ of habeas corpus, the traditional safeguard against unjust imprisonment. It could pass no bill of attainder, a conviction and punishment for a crime by legislative act rather than by judicial process. It could pass no ex post facto law, that is, it could not, by passing a new law, make the position of persons accused of crime, less favorable than when the crime was committed. It could not deny to those who broke its laws a trial by jury. And finally, it could punish for treason only under carefully defined restrictions.

"Three other clauses protected civil liberty from state interference. No state might pass a bill of attainder; it could not pass an ex post facto law; it could pass no law impairing the obligation of contracts. In addition, the states were directed to give to the citizens of each state the privileges and immunities of citizens in the several states. This was to prevent the citizen of a state from being treated like a foreigner when he went into other states." (from New Threats to American Freedoms, by Robert Cushman, Public Affairs Pam-

48

phlet No. 143).

Of all these guarantees of personal liberty that predated the Bill of Rights, the most important is the privilege of the writ of habeas corpus. This is a writ by which a person who is being restrained of his liberty may secure a determination by a judge whether such restraint is proper. In a case arising during the Civil War, the Supreme Court held that a writ may be suspended only when martial law has been declared and the courts are actually closed. Mere existence of a state of war is insufficient to justify suspension of the writ.

Habeas corpus is not a substitute for an appeal, but is limited only to those situations in which the individual has no other means of judicial review. For example, an alien who is detained for deportation may sue out a writ of habeas corpus to have a judicial review of the legality of his detention.

In recent years, the Supreme Court has broadened the scope of the writ. It is now considered an appropriate remedy where a conviction in a state court has been in disregard of the constitutional rights of the accused, and where the writ is the only effective means of preserving those rights. The reasoning behind this is that where constitutional rights are violated, a court loses jurisdiction in the course of a trial. On the other hand, the Supreme Court has also held that where an individual's rights can be completely protected through appeal, he cannot fail to appeal his conviction and then subsequently bring habeas corpus to question the legality of his detention.

Searches and Seizures--The Fourth Amendment

The people have the right to be secure in their persons, houses, papers, and effects against unreasonable searches and seizures. Warrants shall issue only on probable cause and shall describe the place to be searched and the persons or things to be seized. So states the Fourth Amendment.

In general, an officer can make an arrest only with a warrant. If a crime is committed in his presence, however, an officer can make an arrest on the spot without a warrant. An officer may not, however, conduct a search without a warrant and then make an arrest on the basis of what he finds. Under these

49

circumstances, the search, the seizure and the arrest are all unlawful.

Following a lawful arrest, the officer has the right to search the person of the prisoner and to seize those articles found on his person which are connected with the crime. The articles seized may be either the instruments of the crime, i.e. a gun in a robbery, or the spoils of the crime, i.e. stolen jewels. The officer may not seize papers which are evidence of the crime without a warrant.

In the absence of a warrant, the premises in which the prisoner is taken into custody may not be searched. However, visible articles which are instruments of the crime may be seized where there has not been sufficient time for the officer to secure a warrant. During Prohibition, for example, the police were privileged to seize bootlegged liquor in automobiles without a warrant, the courts taking into consideration the fact that a car could make a speedy getaway before a warrant could be secured. But the seizure of illegal distilling apparatus without a warrant although incident to a lawful arrest, was held invalid, where there had been sufficient time to procure a warrant.

For a search warrant to be issued, there must be more than suspicion of crime. A warrant will issue only upon probable cause. Moreover, it must describe specifically the premises to be searched. "Fishing expeditions" and general ransacking of a person's home are forbidden whether the officer acts under the authority of a warrant or without one.

On the other hand, the right of search and seizure with or without warrant is broadened where the articles seized are government property, such as draft cards. The Supreme Court has affirmed the conviction of a person for illegal possession of draft cards which the arresting officer turned up after a five-hour search of the defendant's home. The search warrant had specified only checks allegedly used by the defendant in a series of forgeries. In other words, the Court affirmed conviction for a crime which had been uncovered only as a result of a search not specifically authorized by the search warrant. The Court appeared to be impressed by the fact that draft cards are government property.

In a subsequent case where government property was not involved, the Court retreated from this position, reversing the conviction of a woman who had been arrested without a warrant for conducting an opium den. The conviction was based on the opium which the officers discovered in her hotel room after a limited search. The Court held that there had been ample time for the officers to procure both a warrant for her arrest and a warrant to search her premises.

The Fourth Amendment does not protect the right of privacy generally. Thus the interesting question frequently arises "when is a search not a search?" If an officer uncovers evidence by eavesdropping, he is violating the right of privacy; but the courts have held that he is not violating the Fourth Amendment because he is not trespassing on the person, home, papers or effects of the individual involved. In short, he is not engaged in a "search" within the meaning of the Fourth Amendment. Whenever an officer uncovers crime through his senses, aided or unaided by mechanical gadgets--smell (bootlegged liquor, opium); hearing (eavesdropping, wiretapping, detectaphones), sight (peeping)--the Fourth Amendment is not violated. It is only a trespass on the person or property or access to person or property by fraud or trick that is forbidden by the Fourth Amendment.

Thus evidence which is obtained by some kind of "trespassory incursion" on a person's premises, e.g., the use of a spike mike inserted through a hole drilled in a wall, may not be used at a trial. Where instead of planting the device on the premises, the eavesdropping device is concealed on someone's person, another question is raised to which the court has given no definitive answer. It is clear, however, as a result of the Supreme Court's recent decision in Hoffa v. United States, that if the eavesdropper is someone who the defendant has voluntarily admitted to his presence and consented to talk to, the eavesdropper may himself testify as to what he was told or overheard. Since this is so, presumably any evidence he gathers by using a concealed microphone is also admissible. Such evidence was in fact used to convict a New York State Senator of extortion in 1967.

Since the 1961 decision of the Supreme Court in Mapp v. Ohio, the rule with respect to the admissibility of evidence uncovered by unlawful searches and seizures has been the same in both federal and state criminal prosecutions: the evidence is excluded. With that decision, the Supreme Court made the Fourth Amendment's ban on illegal searches and seizures applicable to the states through the due process clause of the Fourteenth Amendment. The obvious reason for extension of the federal exclusionary rule to the states was to curb police conduct in the various states violative of the Amendment's guarantees (the same motive undergirding other recent extensions of the guarantees of the Bill of Rights to the states through the due process clause of the Fourteenth Amendment). Another reason for extending the exclusionary rule to the states was to prevent federal officers from evading the rule by resort to the "silver platter" doctrine whereby federal officials were premitted to use evidence illegally seized by state officers in federal trials so long as the federal officials were not themselves participants in capturing the evidence.

Not every defendant who is convicted on evidence that has been obtained illegally can invoke the protection of the Fourth Amendment. If there is any suggestion of consent to search and seizure on the part of the defendant, he cannot subsequently challenge its legality even though it would have been unlawful had he not consented. Moreover to invoke the Fourth Amendment, a defendant must be the direct and immediate victim of the unlawful search and seizure. Thus, if tapping the telephone conversations of A and B furnishes evidence of crime committed by C, C cannot secure a reversal of his conviction by resort to the Fourth Amendment.

WIRETAPPING, BUGGING, AND EAVESDROPPING: Though the courts and commentators have distinguished wiretapping (the interception of telephonic communications from other kinds of eavesdropping (e.g. bugging, the use of electronic or mechanical devices for the purpose of overhearing conversations not occurring on the telephone), the search and seizure issue presented is the same, i.e. both practices involve general rather than specific searches as required by the Fourth Amendment. The object to be seized or the premises to be searched cannot be limited or even specified since any eavesdropping device necessarily records whatever utterances are made. The threat to privacy occasioned by wiretapping and the use of modern scientific devices for eavesdropping is apparent. At the same time, law enforcement authorities--from the Department of Justice down to the local constabulary--regard wiretapping and the use

52

of electronic devices as essential to effective crime fighting.

Prior to enactment of the Omnibus Crime Control and Safe Streets Act of 1968, all federal interception and divulgence of telephone conversations was illegal. While the FBI admitted to eavesdropping, it was assertedly limited only to matters of national security. On the state level, the approach was varied and inconsistent--some states forbade wiretapping by officials; some permitted it under restrictions and specific requirements; some had no legislation at all. The Omnibus Crime Control Act authorized eavesdropping at all levels of government, federal and state, for a designated group of suspected crimes, but with the requirement that it be court authorized, except in matters of national security, where the executive branch could authorize without court authorization (i.e. Justice Department). Combined with the wider latitude afforded by the Act, a broadened definition of national security to include domestic political actions "to attack and subvert the government by unlawful means," has broadened substantially the area of legalized wiretapping and eavesdropping.

Prosecution Without Persecution--
The Fifth Amendment

INDICTMENT BY GRAND JURY: The Fifth Amendment requires that prosecution for all "capital or infamous crimes" be instituted by indictment or presentment by a grand jury. This requirement has thus far been held not to apply to the states although if the current trend toward absorption of the Bill of Rights in the Fourteenth Amendment continues, it will eventually be made applicable to the states. Most states though have similar provisions in their state constitutions. In some states, like Louisiana and California, prosecution may be begun by information, i.e. the District Attorney or Attorney General, rather than the grand jury, makes a sworn accusation that the defendant has committed a crime. Michigan has a "one man" grand jury system under which a judge sitting as a grand jury may indict. The same judge who acts as a grand jury may not subsequently preside at the trial.

As to the specific crimes for which indictment is required, they are capital crimes--those which carry the death penalty as punishment--and infamous crimes--those which are punished either by imprisonment in a state penitentiary (as distinguished from a workhouse or county jail) or by sentence to hard labor. Where neither a penitentiary term nor hard labor sentence is involved in the punishment, grand jury indictment is not required.

The Fifth Amendment lists certain exceptions to the requirement of indictment by a grand jury. Army or Navy personnel, accused of committing a capital or infamous crime, need not be indicted by a grand jury; likewise a member of the militia in time of war or public danger. During the Second World War, the Supreme Court decided that persons in the service of the enemy, although not expressly excepted by the language of the Fifth Amendment, need not be indicted by a grand jury but can be dealt with in accordance with military law by a military tribunal.

As to whether a person may waive the right to indictment or presentment by a grand jury, the courts have generally upheld the validity of state statutes authorizing waiver even where the state constitutions guarantee grand jury indictment. New York, however, has ruled that indictment is necessary to give a court jurisdiction to proceed and that a statute authorizing waiver of indictment is unconstitutional.

DOUBLE JEOPARDY: The Fifth Amendment likewise prevents any person from being tried more than once for the same offense. This provision had applied to the federal government only, but with the decision in Benton v. Maryland now also applies to the states. Except for Connecticut, Maryland, Massachusetts, North Carolina and Vermont, each of the state constitutions likewise incorporates this protection.

The major issue in securing this right is the definition of a "first jeopardy." For one thing, it is clear that this provision does not prevent a state from punishing a person for the very same conduct which is also a federal offense. During the Prohibition era, many persons were brought to book under both federal and state laws. Similarly, a criminal prosecution does not bar a civil action and vice-versa.

Where a verdict is reached. As a general rule, it is not double jeopardy to prosecute twice for the same conduct, so long as the crimes are different. Crimes are different unless the evidence required to sustain both is the same. Conviction or acquittal of a crime which includes lesser offenses will generally

54

bar prosecution for the lesser offense. Thus, if a man is prosecuted for rape, he cannot on acquittal be prosecuted for assault with intent to rape. Similarly, conviction or acquittal for a lesser offense bars prosecution for the greater offense which includes it. If a man is convicted of assault with intent to rape, he cannot then be prosecuted for rape. In like manner, prosecution for assault with intent to kill bars prosecution for mayhem; prosecution for petty larceny bars prosecution for robbery.

Where, however, after the first prosecution, a new circumstance, changing the criminal character of the defendant's conduct arises, the defendant may be prosecuted for the greater offense. Assume that a man is convicted of assault with intent to kill, and subsequently, his victim in fact dies, the death being traceable to the assault. The defendant may then be prosecuted for homicide. This is not double jeopardy since, on the first trial, the victim still being alive, the defendant could not have been prosecuted for homicide.

There is even the possibility of prosecution for homicide under these circumstances if the defendant is initially acquitted of assault with intent to kill. For in many states, e.g., Illinois, homicide other than murder in the first degree does not require intent to kill, and so a man might not be guilty of assault with intent to kill and still be guilty of homicide if his victim subsequently dies.

Where a lower court verdict is appealed, reversal of a defendant's conviction does not bar a new trial. However, when the prosecution appeals an acquittal, the majority of states will deny a new trial regardless of errors committed by the trial court.

Before verdict is reached: In interpreting the double jeopardy provision, the courts have laid down the general rule that one is in jeopardy when put upon trial before a court of competent jurisdiction, upon an indictment sufficient to sustain a conviction, and a jury has been impanelled and sworn to try him. Where a person is tried under an indictment for error, he may be indicted again. In like manner, a refusal of a grand jury to indict or the quashing of a proceeding prior to impaneling a jury will not bar subsequent indictment and prosecution.

But once the jury is impanelled, there being no defects in the indictment, the defendant is placed in "first jeopardy." Unless the defense subsequently requests a continuance (postponement) or some urgent necessity stops the trial prior to verdict of conviction or acquittal, any termination prior to verdict will be deemed a bar to a new trial. Urgent necessity sufficient to dispose of the claim of double jeopardy and permit a new trial has been found in the following situations when the term of court ends before a decision is reached, when the jury is unable to agree within a reasonable time, i.e., a hung jury, when a biased judgment is feared, and when persons essential to the proper completion of the trial are excusably absent, i.e. a juror or judge takes ill. The courts, however, have generally refused to find that absence of the prosecution's witness constitutes urgent necessity.

Sentence and Punishment: Double jeopardy may arise in the sentencing of a defendant. Where a judge ordered payment of a fine, he was held debarred from imposing a prison sentence after the fine had been tendered to the court. The statute in question gave the court the power to fine or to imprison but not both.

With reference to double jeopardy in punishment, perhaps the most spectacular case ever to arise involved the unsuccessful electrocution of a convicted Negro in Louisiana. The first electrocution having failed, the Supreme Court held that it was neither a double jeopardy nor cruel and unusual punishment to attempt a second electrocution.

THE PRIVILEGE AGAINST SELF-INCRIMINATION: "I refuse to answer on grounds that it may incriminate or degrade me" is a response which is not available to witnesses with the regularity that one might suppose. Since the 1964 decision of the Supreme Court in Malloy v. Hogan, the Fifth Amendment's privilege against self-incrimination has been binding on the states. Even prior to this change in constitutional doctrine, however, Murphy v. Waterfront Comm. decided at the same time as Malloy also changed the Court's prior doctrine on the transferability of the privilege between the state and federal systems by holding that it protects a state witness under both federal and state law and a witness in a federal court from incrimination of either a state or federal crime. State constitutions except those of Iowa and New Jersey afforded protection both on the federal and state levels.

While the governing clause of the Fifth Amendment reads "no person shall be compelled in any criminal case to be a witness against himself," the courts have applied the privilege against self-incrimination to any proceeding where a witness may incriminate himself by answering a question or giving testimony. Thus, the privilege applies not only in criminal proceedings, but in grand jury investigations, bankruptcy proceedings, statutory proceedings for forfeiture of goods, and even in civil suits where an answer to a question might tend to establish the witness' criminal liability. Where the privilege operates, it is improper for a judge to comment on a refusal to testify. In no case, moreover, may a judge charge that refusal to testify creates a presumption of guilt.

The privilege applies to both oral and written testimony. However, there are a number of situations where the privilege cannot be invoked. Corporations are not protected by the privilege, and the records of a corporation may not be withheld by its officers. Similarly, a public official cannot refuse to produce the public records in his custody.

A fundamental question that has been increasingly posed in recent years is whether the privilege protects private business records required to be kept by statute or administrative regulation. Although the Supreme Court has not yet directly considered the problem, a majority of lower federal courts have held that such records are of a "quasi-public" nature, and therefore beyond the scope of the privilege against self-incrimination. Under these decisions, if a regulation is otherwise valid, it will not be unconstitutional for requiring records to be kept and subsequently produced, even though they may reveal evidence of crime.

Another problem that has become increasingly important in recent years is the operation of the privilege against self-incrimination at legislative investigations. The effect of pleading the Fifth on the reputation of the witness, and his consequent punishment by public opinion have been considered earlier.

There seems to be no doubt that the privilege applies. The issue is whether the privilege can be removed by the operation of an immunity statute, i.e. a statute which protects a witness from criminal prosecution on the basis of his testimony. The Supreme Court has held that an immunity statute merely providing protection against subsequent use of a witness' testimony as evidence in a criminal prosecution against him is insufficient to prevent the operation of the privilege against self-incrimination. Under such a statute, the testimony might furnish clues by which other evidence of crime could then be uncovered, and the witness could then be prosecuted on the basis of such evidence. On the other hand, a statute which grants a witness total immunity from criminal prosecution as to any matter concerning which he testifies has been deemed sufficient to suspend the operation of the privilege against self-incrimination. Such legislation is the Federal Immunity Statute of 1954, which the Supreme Court held valid in 1956.

The privilege against self-incrimination may be waived, and this frequently becomes an important issue in court proceedings. A witness will be answering a series of questions and suddenly find himself confronted with the prospect of confessing to a crime if he answers the next question. The courts have held that the privilege is waived where the witness, by answering some questions, leads himself to the point where the incriminating question is asked. He is expected to foresee the logical course of questioning and to invoke his privilege early in the testimony.

DUE PROCESS: The reader will observe that most of the guarantees of personal liberty contained in the Bill of Rights have been absorbed into the Fourteenth Amendment. The due process clause of the Fourteenth Amendment has grown to the stature of a second Bill of Rights applicable to state governments so as to include most of the specific provisions of the federal Bill of Rights as components of the "fair trial" the states are required to furnish criminal defendants.

What are the elements of due process? In the first place, due process requires that a person receive notice of the charge or claim against him and that, on demand, he be furnished with a bill of particulars specifying the exact nature of such charge or claim. Secondly, due process requires an atmosphere in which a fair hearing can be conducted. There is no "fair trial" where mob feeling is such that lynching is threatened if a prisoner is not convicted. There is no "fair trial" where the judge is prejudiced or where the jury is improperly chosen, i.e. Negroes have been deliberately excluded from jury service where a Negro is on trial. Thirdly, confessions extorted by third degree methods or by fraud and trickery are inconsistent with due process as is perjured testimony. The presence either of extorted confessions or of perjured testimony will require reversal of a conviction regardless of other evidence in the case.

Due process does not include the right to appeal, except that there must be a provision for judicial review where constitutional issues are involved, i.e. by writ of habeas corpus. However, where a state has created an appeals machinery to deprive a person of an appeal is a violation of due process as well as a denial of equal protection of the laws.

Of all the guarantees of personal liberty, due process is probably the most elastic, since it can be made to cover all situations in which minimum standards of fair hearing have not been maintained. Thus, if a state acts with wanton disregard of these guarantees, thereby prejudicing the defendant, the proceeding can be set aside as wanting in due process. This is particularly true where the right to trial by jury and to assistance of counsel under the Sixth Amendment is involved (See infra, pages 55, 57). In Garret v. Arizona, juvenile proceedings were held to require the same tests of due process as pertain to other criminal proceedings.

One of the most important issues of the post-war period has been the applicability of requirements of due process to loyalty hearings. Under one approach, it is argued that there is no "right" to a federal jub, and that loss of a government job is not "punishment" in the legal sense. From this premise it follows that the requirements of due process as they apply to a court trial have no applicability to a hearing to determine the suitability of an individual for federal employment. As late as 1950, the Supreme Court upheld this point of view--although by a margin no greater than a 4-4 split which upheld a 2-1 decision of a lower federal court.

It was not until 1955 that the Court began to reexamine this line of thinking and to extend due process requirements to hearings under loyalty-security executive orders. Actually, in Peters v. Hobby, decided that year, the majority decision avoided the constitutional issue of due process and ordered the reinstatement of Dr. Peters on the grounds that the loyalty review board had exceeded its authority, when it reversed a departmental decision sustaining Dr. Peter's loyalty. The concurring decison by Justice Douglas, however, came to grips with the problem of due process.

In the Jencks case, (1957), the Court held that defendants in criminal cases have the right to examine FBI reports of witnesses who testify against them. This has been variously interpreted in lower courts as meaning the handing over of full investigative reports to defense counsel, sometimes even in advance of going to trial.

The Attorney General and the Director of the FBI subsequently took the position that this decision threatened a breakdown in Federal law enforcement through the compelled exposure of confidential informants and methods of procedure, particularly in counter-espionage cases. Congress later set limits on the Court's decision through legislation protecting the files of the FBI and other Federal agencies from public exposure. However, the Jencks Act (as it has come to be known) does require that statements in the possession of the government shall be made available to the defense insofar as they relate to the testimony of government witnesses.

The cases since Peters seem to indicate that in the loyalty-security area, the Court will review each case on its own factual situation and will not attempt an all-encompassing rule of law. In the Greene case (1959), the security firing of a government engineer was reversed because he had not received a full due process hearing. Yet in Brawner (1960), the Court said, "The Fifth Amendment does not require a trial-type hearing in every conceivable case of government impairment of interest."

In a totally different area, the Supreme Court in the Dixon case (1962) upheld a lower court decision that the expulsion of six Alabama State College students for sit-in activities was an unconstitutional act on the part of the tax-supported college in the absence of a hearing. This would appear to suggest that, in connection with the overall assertion of civil rights (see ahead, Chapter Three) protections afforded by the First, Fifth, and Fourteenth Amendments will take precedence over the so-called police power and public welfare, while in the area of national security, though the equation of the early forties has been somewhat restored, national security will probably continue to enjoy some precedence over individual freedom.

TRIAL BY JURY: The Sixth Amendment requires a speedy and public trial by an impartial jury in the district in which the crime has occurred. This requirement of jury trial applies to the federal government but is not binding on the states, and many of the states dispense with jury trial in prosecutions for minor crimes and misdemeanors. All of the states, however, have constitutional provisions requiring trial by jury for serious crimes.

As to whether trial by jury may be waived, the courts have gradually moved away from their former unyielding insistence on trial by jury where serious crimes are involved. With reference to the federal courts, the Supreme Court has held that partial waiver of jury, in the sense of agreement by defense and prosecution on less than twelve jurors sitting in a criminal case, is permissible. The language in this case has been used by state courts to validate statutes authorizing complete waiver of trial by jury notwithstanding the requirements of state constitutions. New York, by constitutional amendment, authorizes the waiver of trial by jury in all cases where it is agreeable to defense and prosecution.

The more important issue in connection with trial by jury is the requirement that the jury be impartial. For, while trial by jury, in and of itself, is not regarded as an essential element of due process, trial by an impartial jury is a different matter. A partisan or prejudiced jury, or one drawn from lists which exclude certain persons solely because of their race, class, or sex, is a denial of due process and forbidden by the Fifth and Fourteenth Amendments to the Constitution.

The Supreme Court has indicated that it thinks that an impartial jury should be one chosen from a cross-section of the population. However, the Constitution does not secure to an accused person the right to have his race represented on the jury that indicts or tries him. It is only the deliberate exclusion from the jury lists of Negroes, laborers or women that is a violation of due process and a denial of equal protection of the laws. Accordingly, when the prosecution rejects all Negroes on the jury list, in the exercise of its privilege to reject up to twenty jurors without giving any reason, the courts have held that this is not a violation of due process. But in a 1965 Alabama case, the Supreme Court intimated that if the prosecutor in a given county in a state, systematically rejects all Negroes on a jury list in all cases, year after year, this would violate the equal protection clause of the Fourteenth Amendment.

Another aspect of the problem of representativeness of the jury is the legality of so-called "blue ribbon" juries, i.e., juries selected from lists composed of persons presumed to be more competent, more intelligent and less prejudiced than ordinary jurors. "Blue ribbon" juries are legal in eight states--Alabama, Michigan (Detroit only), New Jersey, New York (New York City only), Tennessee (civil cases only), Vermont, Virginia (civil cases only).

In most states where it is permitted, a "blue ribbon" jury may be granted on a motion of either party where the court is convinced that the importance or intricacy of the case demands or efficient and impartial justice requires it. In other words, the granting or denial of a "blue ribbon" jury is almost wholly discretionary with the trial court.

In New York, the "blue ribbon" jury is picked from the list of ordinary jurors by the county clerk. Each juror is personally interviewed and required to swear that he has no scruples against the death penalty, no such preformed opinion that he is unable to lay it aside, and no prejudice against particular laws or defenses. In a recent case before the Supreme Court, two labor leaders charged with extortion challenged the validity of the New York "blue ribbon" jury system on the grounds that workers and women had been purposely excluded from the jury lists and that "blue ribbon" juries have a greater tendency to convict than do ordinary juries.

In a split decision, the Court upheld the "blue ribbon" jury, deciding that is is neither a violation of due process nor a denial of equal protection of the laws. The Court found no deliberate or systematic exclusion of workers, and found nothing wrong with the New York rule permitting women to claim exemption from both ordinary and "blue ribbon" juries.

Actually, the uniformly higher quality of ordinary juries is gradually outdating the "blue ribbon" jury. Pennsylvania abolished its "blue ribbon" jury system in 1937, and Massachusetts defeated a bill that would have authorized "blue ribbon" juries. New York, by a recent statutory amendment, set the same qualifications for ordinary jurors as for "blue ribbon" jurors.

The question of service by women on juries is a vital part of the concern that jurors be representative and impartially selected. Though there are more women than men in the nation, outmoded concepts of a woman's "place" have been reflected in our laws relating to their rights to serve on juries. Not until 1957 were women allowed to serve on federal juries. Two states, Mississippi and South Carolina, still prohibit service by women altogether as did Alabama until last year, when a federal district court held its law unconstitutional. Of the 48 states which permit jury service by women, many make such service voluntary rather than required as in the case of men, and the Supreme Court has upheld these laws. There is no good reason for treating men and women differently with respect to jury service; to the extent that their opportunity to serve is the same, to that extent is the administration of justice fairer.

ADVICE OF COUNSEL: "Say nothing until you talk to me!" is the first advice of the criminal lawyer to his client who has just been booked on criminal charges. A person accused of crime, where he can afford counsel, will spare no expense to get the best lawyer in town. For, he recognizes that a good lawyer is his best protection. Yet a great number of persons charged with crime, ranging all the way from minor offenses to first degree murder, are often too poor to engage the services of a lawyer to defend themselves properly. What protection does our system offer these people?

"In all criminal prosecutions, the accused shall enjoy the right . . . to have the assistance of counsel for his defense." So reads the Sixth Amendment to the Constitution which until 1963 applied only to the federal government. But in that year, the Supreme Court, in the landmark case of Gideon v. Wainwright, unanimously held that this provision of the Bill of Rights was obligatory on the states through the Fourteenth Amendment. As a consequence of Gideon, the distinction between the right to counsel in capital (death penalty) and non-capital cases was erased as was the distinction--at least with respect to all felonies (cases punishable by imprisonment in a penitentiary or for more than one year)--between criminal cases in the federal and state courts.

63

It is still true, however, that the right to counsel in federal courts is somewhat broader than is the right in state courts because the Supreme Court has not yet declared that persons charged in those courts with misdemeanors (less serious crimes) have the right to the appointment of a lawyer. This is true in the federal courts. Though the Supreme Court has thus far declined to extend the right of counsel to misdemeanants in state courts, at least three of its justices (Justices Stewart, Black, and Douglas), recognizing that this question was left unanswered by Gideon, indicated in two cases, during a recent term of the Court, a desire to have the Court clarify this question. In the meantime, however, some lower federal courts have not hesitated in applying the Gideon rule to misdemeanor cases. The Fifth Circuit Court of Appeals (covering the Deep South) has ruled in two cases--one involving a sentence of six months, the other of ninety days--that counsel must be appointed by the state for an indigent. This court has refused to recognize any "petty offense" exemption to the rule. Similarly, a federal district court in Connecticut has ruled that the failure of that state to apprise a misdemeanant of his right to appointed counsel and to offer to secure counsel for him if requested, violated his right to due process under the Fourteenth Amendment.

To the extent that there is a difference between a serious misdemeanor and a "petty offense," or something less than a serious misdemeanor, the courts are presented with still another question as to the scope of the Gideon rule. Title 18, Section 1 (3) of the United States Code defines a petty offense as "any misdemeanor, the penalty for which does not exceed imprisonment for a period of six months or a fine of not more than $500 or both . . ." Congress, in enacting the Criminal Justice Act of 1964 providing for the appointment of counsel for indigents in the federal courts, has recognized this statutory distinction and has not required such appointment in the case of petty offenses. The reasoning behind this is obviously to prevent imposing on the courts the extremely heavy burden that a requirement of appointed counsel in every case would be. But certainly the logic of Gideon extends this far as does manifestly the force of the constitutional principle. And as indicated above, at least one appellate federal court sees no occasion for not extending the guarantee to petty offenses.

What is the scope and practical effect of the right to counsel at trial in those cases in which, since Gideon, it has been clearly established. First, the accused must be advised of the right at the preliminary examination or arraignment and given an opportunity to secure counsel of his choosing or to have one appointed by the court. Second, a plea of guilty at arraignment (where an accused pleads to the charge) does not of itself constitute a waiver of the right. The right, of course, may be waived but there must be other satisfactory evidence that the accused knowingly and intelligently waived the right. Nor does the failure to request counsel constitute a waiver if the right exists. Third, the right to counsel means effective assistance of counsel and requires that counsel be competent, that there be opportunity to confer privately with and receive the advice of one's counsel, that there be opportunity for counsel adequately to prepare the defense, and that there be opportunity for counsel to present the case without interference or prejudice.

RIGHT TO COUNSEL DURING CUSTODIAL INTERROGATION: The most dramatic and important extension of the right to counsel in recent years has occurred in the area of interrogation of suspects by the police during pre-trial custody. The rules were announced in two cases decided two years apart, Escobedo v. Illinois (1964) and Miranda v. Arizona (1966), and they have had a revolutionary effect on law enforcement methods and procedures.

In Escobedo, the Supreme Court held that the confession of a suspect obtained by the police as a result of interrogation at the police station while denying the suspect's request to consult his attorney and preventing his attorney who had come to the police station from consulting him could not be used in evidence. In Miranda, the court expanded the doctrine of Escobedo to all situations in which a police investigation has focused on an individual as a suspect and he is deprived of his "freedom of action in any significant way," i.e., by custodial restraint. In the course of its opinion in Miranda, the Supreme Court, for the first time enunciated specific rules for law enforcement agencies governing the procedure during custodial interrogation. A statement of these rules makes clear that the Court was concerned with safeguarding the Fifth Amendment privilege against self-incrimination made applicable to the states by Malloy v. Hogan (see supra, p.50) and that a majority of the Court deemed it essential that the Sixth Amendment's guarantee of the right to counsel be invoked as one of the means for safeguarding this privilege. In Orozco v. Texas, the Court held that admissions obtained from a suspect in his bedroom, when Miranda warnings had not been given, could not be introduced in evidence.

As stated by Chief Justice Warren, the rules governing interrogation by the police of criminal suspects are: (1) "the suspect must be warned that he has a right to remain silent;" (2) "that any statement he does make may be used as evidence against him;" (3) "that he has a right to the presence of an attorney, either retained or appointed;" (4) "if . . . he indicates in any manner and at any stage of the process that he wished to consult an attorney before speaking there can be no questioning;" (5) "if the individual is alone and indicates in any manner that he does not wish to be interrogated, the police may not question him." These rights may be waived, but the waiver must be "made voluntarily, knowingly and intelligently." Unless such procedure is followed, no evidence obtained during an interrogation can be used at trial.

OTHER RIGHTS OF DEFENSE: Under the Sixth Amendment, a defendant has the right to be confronted with the witnesses against him and to have compulsory process (subpoena) to bring forth the witnesses in his favor. A 1965 Supreme Court decision made this provision expressly applicable to the states thus continuing the process of absorption of the Bill of Rights in the Fourteenth Amendment. On trial, both the prosecution and the defense have the right to cross-examine each other's witnesses. As previously noted (see p.39), this issue has been involved in loyalty hearings.

Neither the prosecutor nor the judge can comment on the defendant's failure to testify at his trial; this would subvert the protection of the privilege against self-incrimination. And prejudicial publicity (Sheppard v. Maxwell--1966) or the use of television during the trial (Estes v. Texas--1965) vitiate the defendant's right to a fair trial.

The Eighth Amendment protects a person charged with crime from excessive bail and fine and from cruel and unusual punishment. This provision of the Bill of Rights is also applicable to the states. While, in general, the courts will not review the figure at which bail is set, discrimination in the setting of bail or fine is forbidden.

Rights After Conviction of a Crime

Simultaneous with the expansion of the Bill of Rights guarantees during pre-trial and trial proceedings has been the development of legal safeguards for the protection of the basic rights of persons after they have been convicted of a crime. Many persons assume erroneously that once a man is convicted of a crime he has no further legal rights. This is not true. There are two areas in which there have been noteworthy developments in this field.

POST CONVICTION REMEDIES: Increasingly, the federal courts have expanded the federal habeas corpus jurisdiction to permit state prisoners to raise a variety of claims of the deprivation of constitutional rights during state criminal proceedings. Ths kind of claims that can be raised run the gamut of all the protections that the Bill of Rights affords. As enunciated by the Supreme Court, the most important feature of the expanded federal habeas corpus jurisdiction is the rule of Townsend v. Sain, a case decided in 1963, which requires the federal district courts to grant evidentiary hearings to state prisoners alleging a deprivation of their constitutional rights in circumstances where the claim has not been adequately ventilated during the course of state proceedings. An important cognate development is the rule of the Supreme Court in Sanders v. United States which vests the district courts with discretion to entertain repeated claims that may have been urged before in a previous application for the federal writ. The underlying purpose for this expansion of doctrine is to assure that the ends of justice are served and that no prisoner remains incarcerated pursuant to a conviction that was obtained in a manner forbidden by the Constitution.

In addition to the federal post-conviction remedy, several state legislatures have enacted statutes providing for post-conviction review by their state courts of federal constitutional claims. These include Illinois, Nebraska, Maryland, North Carolina,

Maine, Oregon, Wyoming, Arkansas, and Florida. Some states have provided post-conviction remedies by rule of court. Among these are Alaska, Delaware, Kentucky, Missouri, and New Jersey. The Supreme Court in a 1965 case urged the states to provide some post-conviction relief for state prisoners thereby relieving the federal courts of the ever-increasing burden of habeas corpus litigation.

RIGHTS OF PRISONERS: Although persons convicted of crimes lose many of the rights and privileges of law-abiding citizens, they do not lose all their civil rights. The due process and equal protection clauses of the Fourteenth Amendment follow them into prison and there provide them some protection from unconstitutional administrative action by prison officials. Specifically, prison authorities are not permitted to inflict cruel and unusual punishment on convicts for violation of prison rules. They may not deny a prisoner reasonable access to the courts to test the validity of his confinement or to secure judicial protection of his constitutional rights. Neither may prison authorities, under the guise of enforcing discipline, discriminate on racial or religious grounds.

The most litigated issue of the present day involves the practice of their religion by Negro prisoners who are members of the Black Muslims, as this group is popularly known. Because of the unpopularity of members of this group, prison authorities have on occasion attempted to restrict the right of Black Muslim prisoners to hold services while confined to jail or to otherwise practice their religion. However, several federal cases have made clear that Black Muslims, no less than Protestants, Catholics or Jews, have a constitutional right to practice their religion while behind bars so long as such religious observance does not undermine the exercise of legitimate disciplinary authority. The difficulty in most of the cases is that of drawing the line between those activities which are the legitimate free exercise of religion and those which prison officials may forbid on grounds of prison discipline.

Conclusion

In making a reality of the guarantees of personal liberty

contained in the Bill of Rights and of the due process clause of the Fourteenth Amendment, the state courts and the United States Supreme Court have had the problem of pointing a path to freedom for those who are the victims of ignorance and injustice while, at the same time, not opening the gates of our jails for hardened criminals. The growing tendency is to view each case on its particular facts, to ascertain whether fundamental concepts of justice and fairness have governed. While this approach makes for some uncertainty in the administration of law, it is perhaps the surest way to protect both the rights of the accused and the rights of the community. Recent developments to be pointed out are the trend toward applying the requirements of fair trial into the twilight area of legislative investigations and loyalty hearings even though these are not precisely criminal in nature, and the almost complete molding of the specific provisions of the Bill of Rights to the frame of the Fourteenth Amendment, thereby requiring more responsibility from the states for the protection of fundamental liberties.

On the other hand, the legislatures both Federal and state, presumably responding to the public outcry for "law and order," appear prepared to curtail certain of the judicially construed liberties. New York's "stop and frisk" law (defeated in Michigan and Illinois), and upheld by the state's highest court, permits search without warrant where there is "reasonable suspicion" of crime, a lesser test than the judicial criterion of "probable cause." In Congress, so-called "no knock" legislation has been enacted for the Dictrict of Columbia (possibly a preliminary to a federal enactment that would cover the nation) which permits federal agents to break in without notice and to conduct exploratory searches without warrant where suspicion of narcotics violation is involved.

Congress' restrictive attitude was first reflected in the Omnibus Crime Control and Safe Streets Act of 1968, in which the original bill proposed by the Justice Department under Attorney-General Ramsey Clark was substantially amended prior to passage to widen the authority of federal crime officers. The Anti-Riot Act, previously referred to, and since its enactment in 1968 the base of the Chicago 7 trial, was further reflective of a more repressive attitude, as the federal government, for the first time, moved legislatively into the area of riot. More recently, proposed preventive detention legislation has been under consideration. This legislation would authorize judges to jail individuals charged with alleged violent crimes prior to their trial without the right to release on bail or personal recognizances.

The appearance of new methods of police surveillance, increased computerization of personal data and information, liberalized wiretapping rules at the federal level-- all implicit threats to the right of privacy -- add to the growing move toward less protection for traditional personal liberty, despite broadened judicial protection of these liberties on a case-by-case basis. Whether these legislative efforts will have the desired effect of reducing the alarming crime rate in the country remains to be seen. Traditional advocates of civil liberties see a threat to constitutional rights without compensating benefits in public welfare.

Chapter III
SUMMARY OF THE PRIVACY ACT OF 1974

The Provisions

Coverage: The major portion of the Act which became effective on September 27, 1975, applies only to the federal government and covers all executive departments, the military, independent regulatory agencies, government corporations, and government-controlled corporations such as the Federal Reserve Banks and the Federal Home Loan Corporation. 5 U.S.C. 552a(a) (1) and 552(e). (All subsequent citations will be to 5 U.S.C.) It does not apply to Congress, the governments of United States territories or possessions, the District of Columbia, or the federal courts. It is not certain whether it covers court-martial records.

If a federal agency contracts with a private business or state or local government to run the agency's record system, the contractor's employees are considered to be the agency's employees. #555a(m).

The term "record" is defined broadly as "Any item, collection or grouping of information about an individual that is maintained by an agency, including, but not limited to, his education, financial transactions, medical history, and criminal or employment history and that contains his name, or the identifying number, symbol, or other identifying particular assigned to the individual, such as a finger or voice print or photograph." #552a(4).

The Act uses the phrase "system of records" to define a group of records from which information can be retrieved by using an individual's name or other identifying particular. #552a (5). The term "statistical record" means a record in a system of records used for research or reporting purposes and not for making determinations about individuals. Census data is excepted from this definition. #552a(6).

Data Collection

An agency must inform in writing each individual from whom it requests information concerning:

- The authority under which the information is solicited;
- Wheteer disclosure is mandatory or voluntary;
- The principal purposes for which the information will be permitted to be used;
- The routine uses that may be made of the information; and
- The effects on him if the information is not provided.

To the greatest extent practicable, it must collect information directly from the individual whose rights, benefits, and privileges under Federal programs may be extremely affected by the information. #552a(e)(2) and (3).

data retention; An agency may maintain information about an individual only if it is "relevant and necessary to accomplish" an agency purpose required by law. #552a(e)(1). An agency must keep records used by it to make determinations about an individual "with such accuracy, relevance, timeliness, and completeness as is reasonably necessary to assure fairness to the individual." #552a(e)(5).

Records cannot be kept that describe an individual's exercise of first amendment rights unless a statute or the individual himself authorizes the keeptng of the record, or the record is pertinent to and within the scope of an authorized law enforcement activity. #552a(e)(6).

Data Disclosure

An agency may not disclose "by any means of communication" any record to any person or another agency. #552a(b). Disclosure may be made:

- Upon the written consent of the individual to whom the record pertains;
- To the agency personnel who need the information to perform their duties;
- When required by the Freedom of Information Act, 5 U.S.C. #552;
- For a purpose compatible with the purpose for which it was collected;

72

- To the Bureau of the Census, for planning or carrying out a census survey;
- For statistical research, in a form that is not individually identifiable;
- To the National Archives, if the record has a sufficient historical value, or to the Administration of General Services for a determination of historical importance;
- Upon a written request specifying the portion of the record sought and the law enforcement activity involved, to an agency or instrumentality of any governmental jurisdiction in the United States for a civil or criminal law enforcement activity authorized by law;
- When the health or safety of the individual is involved, providing that notification of disclosure is sent to the individual's last known address;
- To Congress or to any congressional committee with jurisdiction over the subject matter;
- To the Comptroller General in the course of performance of his duties; and
- Pursuant to a court order, if reasonable efforts to notify the individual involved are made once the legal process becomes a matter of public record. See #522a(e)(8).

Before an agency discloses an individual record to any person other than an agency, unless the disclosure is required by the Freedom of Information Act, it must make reasonable efforts to assure that the record is "accurate, complete, timely, and relevant for the agency's purposes." #522a(e)(6).

For most of these disclosures, the agency must make and retain for at least 5 years a record of the date, nature, and purpose of the disclosure, and to whom it was made. #522a(c) (1) and (2). This record must be available to the individual named in the disclosure. #522 a(c)(3).

An agency must permit an individual access to his record or information about him, and an opportunity to make a copy. #522a(d)(1). He may be denied access to any information compiled in reasonable anticipation of a civil action or proceeding. #522a(d)(5).

Data Amendment

An individual may request amendment of a record about him. This request must be acknowledged within 10 days of receipt. Then either the correction must be made, or he must be

73

notified of the refusal of the request and the reasons therefor and of the procedures for a review of the refusal. He may appeal the refusal to amend his record, and a final determination must be made, normally within 30 working days.

If still dissatisfied, the individual may seek judicial review in the Federal District Court and he may file with the agency a concise statement indicating the reason for his disagreement. Thereafter, this statement of disagreement must accompany that portion of the record that he disputes. #552a(d)(2), (3) and (4). The agency must also inform those to whom a recorded disclosure was made of any corrections or disagreements by the individual with the accuracy of the record. #552(c)(4).

Data Protection

An agency "must establish appropriate administrative, technical, and physical safeguards to insure the security and confidentiality of records." #552a(e)(10). It must also establish rules of conduct for persons involved in the operation and maintenance of any system of records. #552a(e)(9).

Exemptions

The heads of some agencies may establish rules, in accordance with the Administrative Procedure Act, that exempt any record system in their agency from the provisions that individuals have access to their records and the data be collected in accordance with Privacy Act's specifications. The agency head can also exempt a system from some of the Privacy Act's provisions for accuracy and criminal penalties for non-compliance. These exemptions are permitted only if the record system is maintained either by the Central Intelligence System or by an agency whose principal activity is in the criminal justice field and the records consist of information identifying individual offenders or are compiled for the purpose of a criminal investigation or about an individual at any criminal law enforcement stage. #552a(j).

Furthermore an agency head may also by rule exempt certain record systems from the Privacy Act's requirements that:

- The identity of those who examined an individual's records be disclosed;
- An individual have access to his records;
- Only relevant information be retained;

- Agency procedures for individual access and information be published annually; and
- The agency establish rules for individual access. #552a (k).

These exemptions apply only to records that are:

- Classified as secret in the interests of national defense and foreign policy;
- Composed of investigatory material required for law enforcement purposes, unless the information will lead to a denial of an individual's right or privilege under federal law;
- Maintained in connection with the protection of government personnel by the Secret Service;
- Required by statute to be maintained solely for statistical purposes;
- Investigatory data compiled for the purpose of determining suitability for federal employment, military service, contracts, or access to classified material, but only insofar as disclosure would reveal the identity of the government's source;
- Testing and examination materials used to determine qualifications for employment or promotion, if disclosure would compromise the objectivity of the testing process; and
- Materials used to evaluate promotion potential in the Armed Services to the extent that access would disclose a source that gave information under a promise of confidentiality.

The Freedom of Information Act also contains a number of exemptions to its disclosure requirements. These exemptions include classified material, personnel medical files, and specified investigatory records. Realizing that an agency might rely on these exemptions to withhold an individual's record, Congress specifically provided that Freedom of Information Act exemptions cannot be used to withhold a record from an individual that is accessible to him under the Privacy Act. #552a(q).

Public Notice

Every agency must publish annually in the Federal Register a notice of the existence and character of the system of records it maintains. The notice must include information about:

- The name and location of the system;
- The type of individuals on whom records are maintained;
- The categories of the records in the system;
- Each routine use of the records, including the categories of users and why they use it;
- The agency's policies and practices regarding the storage, retrievability, access controls, retention, and disposal of records;
- The title and address of the agency official responsible for the system;
- The procedure by which the individual can request notification if the record system contains information on him;
- How an individual can obtain access to his record and contest its contents; and
- The categories of sources of records that are in the system. #552a(e)(4).

Before establishing or altering a record system, an agency must notify both Congress and the Office of Management and Budget sufficiently in advance to permit them to evaluate the "probable or potential effect of such proposal on the privacy or other personal or property rights of individuals or the disclosure of information relating to such individuals, and its effect on the preservation of the constitutional principles of federalism and separation of powers." #552a(o).

In addition, agencies must publish a notice of any new use or intended use of the information in their systems in the Federal Register, and give interested persons an opportunity to submit comments. #552a(e)(11).

Civil Remedies

Any agency may be civilly sued in the United States District Court in the district in which the complainant resides or has his place of business or the agency records are situated, or the District of Columbia, if it:
- Refuses an individual access to his records;
- Refuses to amend an individual's record in accordance with his request, or fails to review the denial;
- Fails to maintain an accurate, relevant, timely, or complete record about an individual who is adversely affected thereby; or

76

- Fails to comply with any provision of the Act or any rule promulgated thereunder in a way that adversely affects any individual. #552a(g)(1).

The District Court determines the matter de novo. It may order the agency to produce or amend a record and to pay attorney and litigation fees where the complainant has substantially prevailed. #552a(g)(2)(3), and (5).

Where the agency action was intentional and willful and affected the individual adversely, he may recover his actual damages, but in no case less than $1,000, as well as attorney fees and costs. #552a(g)(4).

Criminal Penalties

Agency personnel are guilty of a misdemeanor and subject to a maximum fine of $5,000 if they willfully:

- Disclose information in violation of Act knowing that the disclosure is prohibited; or
- Maintain a system of records without publishing annually in the Federal Register a notice of the existence and character of the system.

Any person who knowingly and willfully requests or obtains any record about an individual under false pretenses is similarly punished. #552a(i).

Mailing Lists

An individual's name and address may not be sold or rented by an agency unless specifically authorized by law. #552a(n).

The Privacy Protection Study Commission

Section 5 of the Privacy Act establishes a seven member Privacy Protection Study Commission, which is required to:

- Study data banks, automated data processing programs, and information systems of governmental, regional and private organizations, in order to determine the standards and procedures in force for the protection of personal information; and
- By June 10, 1977, recommend to the President and Congress the extent, if any, to which the requirements and

principles of the Privacy Act should be applied to the information practices of those organizations by legislation, administrative action, or voluntary adoption.

Conclusion

The Privacy Act seeks to permit an individual to determine what information and records about him are being collected, maintained, used, and disseminated by the Executive Branch of the federal government, and to assure their correctness and completeness. It is one response to the common fear of undue surveillance and interference by "Big Brother." Because it is a reaction to fear of privacy invasion, further congressional and state legislation with reference to the private sector, is very likely.

H.R. 1984

The Privacy Protection Study Commission issued its report in July, 1977. The Commission made 162 recommendations for reform. Congressmen Barry M. Goldwater, Jr., and Edward I. Koch (who became Mayor of New York City while the bill was pending) introduced legislation in the House of Representatives which reflects much of the Commission's report. Rep. Goldwater himself was a member of the Commission. The bill is numbered H.R. 1984. The initials, of course, stand for House of Representatives. The numbers stand for George Orwell's chilling novel about a technologically advanced society in which individual privacy and dignity have been eliminated by a tyrant known as Big Brother. The bill's official title is the Comprehensive Right to Privacy Act.

When Congressman Goldwater was asked if this kind of legislation should not be left to the states, he replied:

> Judging from the response we in Congress are receiving, protection against computerized invasions of privacy is being demanded all across the nation. So if the Federal government doesn't act in this area, you're going to see a host of conflicting legislation adopted by the 50 states. In our computerized age such conflicting regulations would jeopardize the smooth flow of commerce. If we're going to have government regulations in this area, we'll need a standard that's national.

And, when you consider the threat to privacy posed by unregulated computer technology, we must consider government regulations in order to safeguard the rights and liberties of the individual.

While at the time of publication of this volume the Comprehensive Right to Privacy Act was still pending in the legislative process, there is little question that there will be significant privacy legislation in the very near future. A Harris poll in March, 1977, indicated that Americans clearly want action. Three out of four voters back laws that would "lay down rules for the way business and other private organizations should deal with information about individuals."

Chapter IV
CIVIL RIGHTS

May, 1954, marked the date of the momentous Supreme Court decision declaring segregation of the races in public schools unconstitutional. While this case is regarded as a milestone in the history of American constitutional law, it has been significant not only for itself, but for the fact that it ushered in a period of some 15 years in which "civil rights" emerged as the most important social issue of our times. This period has witnessed significant court decisions and legislation which had the simultaneous effect of expanding the legal structure of civil rights protection and eroding the legal structure of segregation. At the same time, social action techniques--boycotts, bus strikes, freedom rides, sit-ins and, in more recent years, militant protest and demonstrations--utilized to dramatize the fight for civil rights have themselves created legal issues involving the limitations on freedom of expression. Thus, considerations of civil rights and civil liberties have become increasingly paired, as was true in the 1930's when the assertion of the rights of organized labor likewise produced a series of civil liberties issues, ranging from picket lines on the one side to employer free speech on the other.

I. THE ROLE OF THE FEDERAL GOVERNMENT

Though Congress, in 1964 and 1968, enacted civil rights legislation more far-reaching than anything enacted at the federal level in nearly a hundred years, the major responsibility for the protection of civil rights in this period has fallen principally on the Supreme Court of the United States and on the legislatures of the states outside the South. The reason for this has been the view held heretofore that the power of the federal government is limited under the "Civil Rights" Amendments to the Constitution--

81

the Thirteenth, Fourteenth and Fifteenth Amendments.

The Thirteenth Amendment abolishes slavery. The Fourteenth Amendment contains three specific prohibitions: (1) no state shall abridge the privileges and immunities of citizens of the United States; (2) no state shall deprive any person of life, liberty or property without due process of law; (3) no state shall deny to any person the equal protection of the laws. The Fifteenth Amendment assures that the right to vote shall not be denied or abridged by the United States or by any state on account of race, color or previous condition of servitude. Each Amendment empowers Congress to enact enforcing legislation and the question which continues to be debated is whether such legislation can constitutionally reach the conduct of private individuals. The Anti-slavery Amendment (XIII) applies to the federal government, the states and private individuals alike; the Due Process and Equal Protection Amendment (XIV) prohibits only state action; and the Vote Amendment (XV) prohibits only federal and state action. Thus, violation of civil rights by state or federal officers may always be dealt with by federal action. And though, according to traditional interpretation of the scope of the 14th and 15th Amendments, relatively few violations of civil rights by private individuals can be dealt with by the federal government, two 1966 decisions of the Supreme Court (discussed below, p.67) indicate perhaps the erosion of traditional notions of the limitations of federal power to reach private conduct.

It is important, however, to note how the notion grew. In 1875, the Congress passed "An Act to Protect All Citizens in Their Civil and Legal Rights." Under this Act, all persons were held entitled to the full and equal enjoyment of inns, public conveyances, theatres and other places of public amusement. Violation of the Act was a misdemeanor and provision was included for $500 civil damages to be paid by the offender to the person aggrieved.

About eight years after the adoption of this Civil Rights Act, the Supreme Court held it unconstitutional. The Court decided that the Fourteenth Amendment, under which the law had been passed, prohibited only invasions by the states of the rights of individuals, but not the invasion of those rights by other individuals. The Court declared that the regulation of the conduct of individuals toward one another on matters of civil rights was exclusively the job of the states and not the federal government. Thus, the flowering--in a 14th Amendment context--of the "state action" doctrine and its cross-pollination to interpretation of the 15th Amendment.

As the Supreme Court developed the "state action" doctrine, however, it has been applied not only to the conduct of state officials, but also to other persons acting under state authority, e.g., a specially deputized sheriff or a store detective empowered by a state statute to make arrests, and to private conduct so intertwined with state conduct or performance as to be indistinguishable therefrom. Thus, for example, in a 1961 case from Delaware, the Supreme Court invalidated racial discrimination by the private lessee of a restaurant located in a parking garage erected as part of a state plan to provide off-street parking facilities on the theory that the parking authority as a state agency was involved in a significant way with the racial discrimination practiced by the private lessee. Likewise, in 1963, a decision by the United States Court of Appeals for the Fourth Circuit held that a private hospital in Wilmington, North Carolina, was exercising a state function by participation in a joint federal-state program for the construction and operation of hospital facilities and, therefore, could not discriminate against Negro physicians or patients. This decision was left intact by the Supreme Court. A year later, a similar decision was made by another Court of Appeals (6th Circuit) in a Nashville, Tennessee case involving a motel which was privately owned and operated but which had been erected on land purchased in a city redevelopment project from a city housing authority with city, state, and federal funds. And in 1966, the Supreme Court held that a park in Macon, Georgia, which had existed in all respects as a public park in the City's "municipal regime" could not discriminate on racial grounds by transferring formal title to the park to private trustees. Thus even though the immediate discriminator is a private person or entity, the state action doctrine has been used by the federal courts to prohibit discrimination in any situation in which a governmental function is performed or there is state control or involvement. Though the "state action" doctrine in terms applies only to the states, the due process clause of the Fifth Amendment has been used by the Supreme Court to enforce a similar non-discriminatory ban on action by the federal government.

The Supreme Court has similarly applied the state action concept to cases arising under the Fifteenth Amendment involving the right to vote. Using the concept, the court has rigorously and systematically struck down all kinds of state schemes such as the "grandfather clause" of state statutes (which stated that Negroes could not vote if their grandfathers had not voted prior to a date when Negroes were disabled from voting), the white primaries, and the use of racial designations on ballots. Whenever these or similar actions were taken by state officials or by so-called private persons who in fact were actually exercising state functions, such discrimination has been held illegal.

But the development of the state action concept under both the Fourteenth and Fifteenth Amendments occurred typically in the context of suits brought by private individuals or private legal organizations, such as the NAACP Legal Defense and Educational Fund, usually seeking to enjoin the practices challenged or on occasion to get damage for the injury caused by the racially discriminatory practices. This was the case for several decades prior to the School Segregation Cases in 1954, and the route of case by case litigation in circumstances in which the private litigants usually had very limited resources made progress painfully slow. Not until the enactment by Congress of the Civil Rights Act of 1957 (see below, p.) did the federal government commit any of its resources to the civil rights struggle--and then only in a limited way in the field of voting. Since then, the role of the federal government in the protection of civil rights has greatly increased. For example, the Civil Rights Act of 1964, the most sweeping piece of federal civil rights legislation since Reconstruction times, added to the authority of the Attorney-General to bring voting rights cases (that had existed since the 1957 Act), the power to bring lawsuits to protect the right of access to privately owned places of public accommodation created by the statute, to bring school desegregation suits on request by individuals in communities, to, in certain limited instances, file lawsuits for the protection of employment rights which were guaranteed for the first time in federal legislation, and to intervene as a plaintiff in any kind of civil rights action initiated by private parties upon certifying that the case is of "general public importance." But perhaps the most potentially far-reaching power given to the federal government by the 1964 Act is that of deferring or withholding funds from a variety of federally financed programs, the benefits of which are found to be denied to persons on racial or religious grounds. This authority was guaranteed pursuant to Title VI of the Act.

All told, the period 1957 through 1968 saw the enactment of five major items of federal civil rights legislation:

The Civil Rights Act of 1957 prohibited action to prevent persons from voting in federal elections, authorizing the Attorney-General of the United States to institute suit when a person was deprived of his voting rights. The Act also set up a Civil Rights Division in the Department of Justice.

The Civil Rights Act of 1960 reenforced the provisions of the 1957 Act as to court enforcement of voting rights, and contained limited criminal penalty provisions relating to bombing and to obstruction of federal court orders.

The Civil Rights Act of 1964 prohibited discrimination in public accommodations and in programs receiving federal assistance. It also prohibited discrimination by employers and unions and created an Equal Employment Opportunities Commission. The Act also strengthened enforcement of voting laws and desegregation of school and public facilities.

The Voting Rights Act of 1965 authorized the Attorney-General to appoint federal examiners to register voters in areas of marked discrimination, and increased penalties for interference with voting rights.

The Civil Rights Act of 1968 prohibited discrimination in the sale or rental of approximately 80% of all housing. It also protected persons exercising specified rights, such as attending school or working. The Act also contained the Anti-riot provisions which have now emerged as the basis for the federal government's efforts to deal with violent demonstrations. While these developments greatly expanded the role of the federal government in the protection of civil rights through the use of civil processes in the courts and administrative regulation, the Congress began in 1969 to take a stricter view of federal legislation in these areas. An effort to equate de jure (enforced by law) segregation in many of the southern states with de facto (a fact of life bred by the existence of Negro ghettoes) segregation in the North sought to require equal enforcement nationally. This effort, supported by the Nixon Administration, has the effect of reducing efforts to desegregate. Similarly, the Voting Rights Act of 1965 has been curtailed in the scope of enforcement. The current attitude suggests a much slower rate of desegregation and related civil rights extensions in the foreseeable future.

Enforcement of Federal Criminal Statutes

There has also been a parallel development with respect to the use of federal criminal statutes primarily through an expansive interpretation by the Supreme Court of two old Reconstruction Era criminal statutes enacted for the protection of civil rights.

SECTION 241--CONSPIRACY TO VIOLATE THE RIGHTS OF CITIZENS: Section 241 of Title 18 of the United States Code is directed against any two or more persons who conspire to interfere with a citizen in the exercise of rights or privileges guaranteed by the Constitution or laws of the United States. The penalty for violation is a fine of not more than $500 or imprisonment for not more than ten years or both. This section seeks to protect a citizen (not merely a resident) against a conspiracy of individuals (they may be either private individuals, public officers, or a combination of both) to deprive him of his constitutional rights.

Until the decisions of the United States Rupreme Court in United States v. Price and United States v. Guest on March 28, 1966, it has been generally assumed that the rights and privileges of citizens guaranteed by the Constitution against interference by private individuals were few in number. For example, it was thought that the basic due process rights spoken of in the Fourteenth Amendment as well as the right to equal protection of the laws were not protected against conspiracy by purely private as opposed to governmental actors. But, on that day, in reviewing the dismissal of two indictments, one of a Mississippi federal grand jury in a criminal prosecution growing out of the murder of three civil rights workers in Philadelphia, Mississippi in June, 1964, and another growing out of the murder of a Washington, D.C., Negro educator traveling through Georgia en route to his home in the same year, the Supreme Court held that Section 241 "embraces all of the rights and privileges secured to citizens by all of the Constitution and all of the laws of the United States." The court specifically held that the federal government may use Section 241 to prosecute the deprivation by private persons of rights derived from the due process clause of the Fourteenth Amendment. The court's decision apparently breathes new life into this statute and it now holds promise for being transformed into an effective vehicle to protect private conspiracies designed to violate civil rights.

Though two of the conspirators in the Price case were state officials (a sheriff and a deputy sheriff), one could construe the court's holding with respect to the question whether Section 241 reaches purely private conduct as a holding that such conduct is reached only in situations where state officials play an active part in the conspiracy. However, in the Guest case, none of the conspirators were state officials, and six judges of the court expressed their view that Section 241 can be used to punish all conspirators interfering with the exercise of Fourteenth Amendment rights whether or not state officials or others acting under color of law are a part of the conspiracy. This expansive interpretation of the scope of this section was made necessary because of the increasing number of cases in the last few years of violence (including the infliction of death) against civil rights workers in the South.

SECTION 242--DENIAL OF RIGHTS UNDER COLOR OF LAW: Section 242 of Title 18 is directed against any person who, under color of law, commits either of two offenses: (a) willfully denies to any inhabitant the rights and privileges guaranteed by the Constitution and federal laws; (b) willfully subjects any inhabitant, on account of his alienage, color or race to different punishments than are prescribed for the punishment of citizens. The section provides a fine of not more than $1,000 or imprisonment for not more than one year or both.

At the same time that the court reinterpreted Section 241, the court also dealt with this section in the Price case. This section formally had been used in prosecutions against law enforcement officers in cases of police brutality such as use of the third degree to extort a confession, beating, or the killing of a prisoner to deprive him of a fair trial. However, the "under color of law" language of the section had generally been interpreted in accordance with the "state action" concept of the Supreme Court discussed above and had, in fact, never been applied to persons who were not state officers. But in United States v. Price, the Supreme Court expanded the scope of this section to permit maintenance of a federal prosecution against private persons who willfully participate in joint activity with the state or its agents in deprivation of civil rights, and made it clear that just as in the case of Section 241 prosecution could be had under this section for violation of any of the rights declared under the federal Constitution.

Thus, in sum, it now seems that the federal government can prosecute under Section 241 any conspiracy of private persons without the requirement that state officials be involved and under Section 242 any private persons who act in concert with state officials.

SECTION 243--DISCRIMINATION IN JURY SELECTION: Section 243 of Title 18 makes it a crime for state officials to discriminate on racial grounds in the selection of jurors. The penalty for violation is a $5,000 fine (no jail sentence). This section clearly applies only to state officials since any person involved in the jury selection process is acting on behalf of the state. However, there has rarely, if ever, been any prosecution under this section. Congress has preferred to get at the problem of racial discrimination in jury selection by affirmative legislation imposing fair jury selection standards in the federal system; the matter of racial discrimination in jury selection in the states has thus far been limited to correction by means of federal court decisions on a case by case basis. These have usually occurred on the review of a criminal conviction where the defendant alleged that the jury which indicted him or which tried and convicted him was illegally constituted because of racial exclusion. (There have, however, been several successful civil suits brought in the federal courts in the last few years to enjoin unconstitutional jury selection procedures.)

Again, in keeping with the increased recognition by the executive and legislative branches of the federal government in the late sixties of the need for federal involvement in civil rights matters, legislation was enacted in the House of Representatives in 1966, which, among other things, would have prescribed procedures designed to assure non-discriminatory jury selection in both state and federal courts. But the legislation failed of passage in the Senate. In 1967, the President again proposed a Civil Rights Bill seeking to prohibit discrimination based on race, color, religion, sex, national origin, or economic status in federal and state jury selections.

PENALTIES: It has long been recognized that the penalties for violation of these criminal statutes are not sufficiently harsh to act as an effective deterrent to the conduct proscribed (in addition to the fact of life that very rarely has the government been able to get convictions in these cases because of biased juries). The relatively mild penalties are out of proportion to the offenses. Hence, part of the subsequent legislation proposed increased penalties for violation of these existing civil rights laws up to life imprisonment where death occurs, and additionally clarified and expanded the specific civil rights for invasion of which a criminal penalty would result. The legislation made it a crime to violate, on the basis of race, color, religion, sex, or national origin, voting rights, the right to run for public office, to serve as a poll watcher, to enroll in or attend a public school or college, to participate in or enjoy any federal or state beneficial program, to seek or engage in employment, to occupy housing, to serve as a juror or to use any public accommodation or facility. The penalties for violation of any of these rights range from a term of years to life imprisonment in cases where death is inflicted.

The Right to Vote

The right to vote in federal elections, i.e., for President, Vice President and Members of Congress, has been construed by the Supreme Court to rest on Article 1, Section 2 of the Constitution. It has also been said that the right inheres in citizens of the Nation as a consequence of their relation with the national government. But under Article 1, Section 2 of the Constitution, whatever qualifications a given state erects for its voters in choosing the state legislature, the same qualifications exist in the states for choosing officers of the federal government.

Negroes, however, despite Article 1, Section 2 of the Constitution were not legally able to vote in national elections until they had been declared citizens of the Nation by Article 1 of the Fourteenth Amendment. (Eleven years before the adoption of that amendment, the Supreme Court had ruled in the Dred Scott Case that Negroes were not citizens of the United States under the Constitution.) And, though Article 2 of the Fourteenth Amendment providing for the diminution of a state's complement of representatives in Congress in the event of a denial to male inhabitants of the states of the right to vote by inference extends to all elections, federal and state, the Fifteenth Amendment was adopted to assure that race, color, or previous condition of servitude would not be one of the qualifications required by the states for participation in voting. (The Nineteenth Amendment, adopted in 1920, similarly prevented the states from continuing the practice of using sex as a qualification for voting.)

The second article of the Fifteenth Amendment gave Congress the power to enforce the Amendment by "appropriate legislation." Congress passed such legislation in 1870, stating that "all citizens of the United States who are otherwise qualified by law to vote in any election by the people in any State . . ." are entitled to vote at all elections "without distinction of race, color, or previous condition of servitude . . ." Congress, however, did not simultaneously enact any legislation providing a specific remedy to enforce this right; there was also no power in the federal government to take enforcement action.

This legislation, codified as Section 1971 of Title 42 of the United States Code, was the only congressional legislation enforcing the provisions of the Fifteenth Amendment until 1957, some 87 years later. In that period, notwithstanding this statute and the Fifteenth Amendment, various devices were used by the southern states to effectively disfranchise Negroes. Even though some of these, such as the "grandfather clause," the "white primaries," the attempt to organize the Democratic Party in the South as a private club and the use of racial designations on ballots were all struck down by the Supreme Court, Negroes were still kept away from the polls by the application of various kinds of literacy tests and by fraud, threats and intimidation. A great deal of this conduct was undertaken by private parties as well as state officials.

But in 1957, the Eisenhower administration, assuming that the problem of racial discrimination against Negroes in the society could be combatted by assuring the right to vote, caused the enactment of the Civil Rights Act of 1957. This legislation added new subsections to Section 1971 of Title 42 declaring illegal intimidation by private parties for the purpose of interfering with the right to vote and authorizing the Attorney General of the United States to sue for injunctive relief against both private parties and state officials in protecting that right. The legislation also elevated the Civil Rights Section of the Criminal Division of the Department of Justice to a Civil Rights Division headed by an assistant attorney general and created a Civil Rights Commission with investigative powers in the field of civil rights. Hence, the United States for the first time was able to bring voting suits in the federal courts to vindicate the Negro's right to vote.

The 1957 Civil Rights Act was amended in 1960 to permit the states themselves to be joined as defendants in voting suits brought against state officials and also authorized an action to proceed against the state if for any reason a particular state official was not available to be sued. The amendment also empowered the district courts, upon finding that a "pattern or practice" of discrimination in voting existed in a community, to register voters on application and provided for the appointment of voting referees to accomplish this. The congressional voting legislation was again amended in 1964 as part of the Civil Rights Act of 1964 to provide that a state official could not apply any qualifications, standards, or procedures to Negro voters different from those applied to other voters in the county; could not deny Negroes the right to vote because of inconsequential errors or omissions on registration applications; nor employ any literacy tests as a qualification for voting unless the test was administered wholly in writing, and the individual given access to a copy of the test and his answers. The amendment also provided that completion of six grades of school would create a presumption of literacy which would avoid the necessity for requiring any separate literacy test.

Notwithstanding the enactment of this voting legislation in 1957, 1960, and 1964, Congress, in 1965, found that Negroes were still effectively disfranchised in the South, and that the case by case process of litigation contemplated under this legislation was simply too slow to be effective. Consequently, it enacted the Voting Rights Act of 1965 which seeks to deal with the problem by making the process of voter registration in the states (registration is a prerequisite to voting in all states) automatic by the use of a "triggering device" for determining when the states may not use literacy tests or other devices to challenge the qualifications of Negroes to vote. The triggering device applies to those states which (1) maintained a test or device, e.g., literacy tests, proof of "good moral character," requirement that a prospective voter must be vouched for by a person already registered to vote as a prerequisite to register for voting as of November 1, 1964, (2) and had a total voting age population of which less than 50% were registered or actually voted in the 1964 Presidential election. If these two factors are present, a state or a part thereof may not use any test or device and in addition is subject to the appointment of federal registrars to register voters. The states covered by the automatic provisions of the 1965 Act are Alabama, Alaska, Georgia, Louisiana, South Carolina, Virginia, and approximately 26 counties in North Carolina. There are criminal and civil penalties for violation of the Act's provisions, and the Attorney General is also authorized to sue for injunctive relief to restrain violations of the Act.

The 1965 Voting Rights Act also directed the Attorney-General of the United States to bring immediate suits in those states still retaining the poll tax to seek a declaration of their unconstitutionality. Previously, the Twenty-fourth Amendment had been adopted in 1964 outlawing the requirement by the states of payment of a poll tax in federal elections. Then, in Harper v. Virginia State Board of Elections, in 1966, the Supreme Court banned Virginia's continued use of the poll tax as a prerequisite for voting in state elections, and subsequent suits brought by the Attorney General in federal courts in Alabama and Texas similarly resulted in outlawing the poll tax so that no vestiges of it now remain. The Supreme Court also in 1966 upheld the constitutionality of the 1965 Voting Rights Act.

As a consequence of this Act, hundreds of thousands of Negroes were added to the voter rolls of several southern states and voted for the first time in 1966. Some Negroes were also elected for the first time to local offices in the southern states. However, experience under the act with respect to election practices on the part of some state officials reveals some continuing resistance to the right of Negroes to exercise the franchise.

In the 1968-69 term, voting and election matters were involved in several opinion cases. A North Carolina county which had maintained segregated and unequal schools was held not entitled, under 4(a) of the Voting Rights Act to reinstatement of a literacy test for voters (Gaston County, N.C. v. U.S.) and changes in Mississippi voting laws were held unenforcible in the absence of federal approval required by Section 5 of the Voting Rights Act of 1965 (Allen v. State Board of Elections). The extension of the Act has been a major issue in Congress in 1969-70 where legislators hostile to the Act are seeking to delimit its coverage to only two states--Georgia and South Carolina--against the seven states to which the Act originally had application. Proponents of extension would ban literacy tests permanently and would extend the Act's application for an additional five years. The Administration, seeking a middle ground, is calling for a nationwide voting rights act.

That voting issues are not limited to the South is evidenced by a 7-2 decision of the Supreme Court, reversing a lower court ruling, and upholding a law permitting thousands of Puerto Ricans to vote in New York on the basis of Spanish literacy. The law, part of the literacy provisions of the 1965 Voting Rights Act, replaced a statute under which New York State had required literacy in English or a sixth-grade education in an English-speaking school as a condition of voting.

II. THE STATES AND CIVIL RIGHTS

In 1954, the locus of civil rights legislation--fair employment practices laws, and laws seeking to protect equality of opportunity in education, housing, and public accommodations--was the Northeast--New York, New Jersey, Massachusetts and Connecticut. The South, on the other hand, existed under a massive code of segregation legislation. By 1970, civil rights legislation had moved substantially across the North and West of the country while, as a result of Supreme Court action, substantial inroads had been made on the legal structure of segregation.

Laws banning racial and religious discrimination in public accommodations now operate in 36 states and the District of Columbia. While the precise wording and coverage of such laws vary from state to state, in general they protect persons against discrimination on account of religious as well as racial difference; and in most cases, they protect the alien as well as the citizen.

These laws exist in Alaska, Arizona, California, Colorado, Connecticut, Delaware, Idaho, Illinois, Indiana, Iowa, Kansas, Kentucky, Maine, Massachusetts, Maryland, Michigan, Minnesota, Missouri, Montana, Nebraska, Nevada, New Hampshire, New Jersey, New Mexico, New York, North Dakota, Ohio, Oregon, Pennsylvania, Rhode Island, South Dakota, Utah, Vermont, Washington, Wisconsin and Wyoming. The passage of laws in Maryland and Kentucky represent the first such in southern states.

Many of the public accommodation laws, frequently referred to as "civil rights laws" go back many years in origin, with the result that they provide for enforcement through civil action for damages, or criminal action initiated by the attorney general's office, or a combination of both. In recent years, it has been realized that administrative, rather than judicial handling of complaints of discrimination, furnishes a more effective remedy. Accordingly, following the earlier lead of Connecticut, Massachusetts, New Jersey, New York and Rhode Island, where an aggrieved party may file complaint with an administrative commission set up to handle all matters of discrimination, Alaska, California, Connecticut, Illinois, Indiana, Iowa, Kansas, Maine, Montana, Nebraska, New Hampshire, Ohio, Oregon, Pennsylvania, Washington and Wisconsin have strengthened their civil rights statutes covering public accommodations.

The following states additionally forbid discriminatory advertising: Colorado, Illinois, Maine, Massachusetts, Michigan, New Hampshire, New Jersey, New York, Pennsylvania, Virginia (religion) and Wisconsin.

In August, 1966, the National Conference of Commissioners on Uniform State Laws promulgated the Model Anti-discrimination Act to encourage uniformity among state laws on the subject and to provide--on the basis of the states' experience with such laws since 1945--examples of things that should be covered in legislation. The Comprehensive Act deals with such questions as racial imbalance in the public schools and discrimination in private schools.

SEGREGATION: Laws compelling segregation of the races in all or some of the places of public accommodation or amusement exist in 13 states--Alabama, Arkansas, Florida, Georgia (still technically), Louisiana, Mississippi, North Carolina, Oklahoma, South Carolina, Tennesses, Texas, Virginia and West Virginia. The extent to which these laws continue to be enforced is doubtful in many of these states, and is under continuing legal challenge in the others.

For example, in 1963, prior to enactment of the Kentucky Public Accommodations Law in 1966, the Governor of Kentucky issued an executive order barring discrimination in public accommodations, and in El Paso, Texas, a local ordinance has been enacted barring discrimination in public accommodations. In Texas, generally, the practice will vary from city to city and from county to county. In West Virginia there appears to have been voluntary acquiescence in court decisions. Throughout the South, in specific areas and in connection with specific facilities, segregation has been ended by judicial fiat. The following is a partial listing of judicial rulings (Federal Courts and Supreme Court) invalidating segregation laws.

--In a series of cases decided in 1963, involving the states of North Carolina and Louisiana and the City of Birmingham, Ala., the Supreme Court ruled that cities and states with segregation laws or official segregation policies may not prosecute Negroes seeking service in private establishments. This decision would appear to render segregation laws unenforceable, though it must be borne in mind that even with the erosion of the legal structure of segregation, local custom will tend to reenforce patterns of segregation. This remains true despite the 1964 federal Civil Rights Act banning discrimination in places of public accommodation.

--In a series of cases in the federal courts and at the Supreme Court level, segregation at airports, on trains and buses, in intrastate as well as interstate commerce, and at facilities associated with transportation terminals, is barred, and segregation signs have been ordered removed. In Bailey v. Patterson (1962), the Supreme Court stated, "we have said beyond question that no state may require racial segregation in interstate or intrastate transportation facilities." It seems apparent, however, that each situation is put to an individual test as southern municipalities and states seek to resist the application of anti-segregation rulings.

--Wherever public funds, whether state or federal, are involved in a public accommodation, segregation is invalid. Thus segregation at public beaches, on public golf courses, in restaurants operated by government facilities, in public parks and playgrounds, in swimming pools and in recreation facilities in scores of cities throughout the South has been outlawed.

SEGREGATION AND BREACH OF PEACE: Since 1955, with the Montgomery, Ala., bus strike, Negroes and whites alike have utilized so-called "non-violent" social action techniques to break down patterns of segregation. Perhaps the most widespread device was the "sit-in" at lunch counters in segregated communities to force an end to the refusal to serve Negroes. Communities have reacted to these and other kinds of direct action demonstrations e.g., marches and picketing by jailing demonstrators for breach of peace.

In 1961, Garner v. Louisiana, the Supreme Court unanimously voided such a conviction for lack of evidence that the demonstrators had disturbed the peace; and in 1963 (Edward v. South Carolina) the Court reversed breach of peace convictions of anti-segregation demonstrators in Columbia, S.C., ruling that Negroes had exercised constitutional rights of free speech and assembly "in their most pristine and classic form."

Similar breach of the peace convictions were overturned in 1965 by the Supreme Court in Cox v. Louisiana but for the first time the Court, in several separate opinions, exhibited some impatience with demonstrations which putatively skirt the borderline of the First Amendment protections of free speech and assembly. In that case, the demonstrators' convictions for picketing near a courthouse were reversed by the narrow margin of 5-4. Again, in Brown v. Louisiana, in 1966, the convictions of Negro demonstrators who sat in a library in Louisiana were narrowly reversed 5-4, by the court. Mr. Justice Black, who wrote the opinion for the four man minority, which included Justices Clark, Harlan and Stewart, expressed the attitude that "it (is) necessary . . . that we stop and look more closely at where we are going" with respect to racial demonstrations. Subsequently, the Court in Adderley v. Florida, decided in October, 1966, affirmed for the first time in several years, the convictions of civil rights demonstrators who were protesting the arrests of other demonstrators on the premises of a county jail in Tallahassee, Florida. The opinion for the now-prevailing five man majority was written by Justice Black.

Thus it seems clear that the Court will invoke the protection of the First Amendment in behalf of civil rights demonstrators, but not without imposing some limitations as to the kind of demonstrations involved.

Equal Opportunity in Employment

FEP LAWS: Until the passage of the employment title of the Civil Rights Act of 1964 (Title VII), the broadest protection against discrimination in employment for reasons of race, color, or religion existed in State Fair Employment Practices legislation (FEP) regulating private employment and creating an administrative machinery for enforcement. Such legislation now exists in 37 states: Alaska, Arizona, California, Colorado, Connecticut, Delaware, Hawaii, Idaho, Illinois, Indiana, Iowa, Kansas, Kentucky, Maine, Massachusetts, Maryland, Michigan, Minnesota, Missouri, Montana, Nebraska, Nevada, New Jersey, New Mexico, New York, Ohio, Oklahoma, Oregon, Pennsylvania, Rhode Island, Utah, Vermont, Washington, West Virginia, Wisconsin and Wyoming. The District of Columbia and Puerto Rico also have FEP laws. At least 41 major municipalities have enacted enforcible fair employment practice ordinances.

HOW FEP WORKS: The following questions and answers based on New York FEP law will serve to describe the basic character and operation of these laws.

What are unlawful employment practices under FEP? (1) for an employer of six or more persons to refuse to employ or to discharge an individual because of race, creed, color or national origin or to discriminate against him in pay or other terms of employment; (2) for a labor organization, because of race, creed color, or national origin, to exclude or expel an individual from membership or to discriminate against its members, an employer or his employees; (3) for an employer of six or more persons or an employment agency in a statement, advertisement, employment application blank or inquiry to express any requirement as to race, creed, color or national origin; (4) for an employer, a labor organization or employment agency to discriminate against an individual because he has instituted or assisted in any proceeding under the law; (5) for any person to aid, incite, or coerce the undoing of any act forbidden by the law.

How is FEP enforced? FEP is generally enforced through a Commission against Discrimination whose members are appointed by the governor. The Commission has the power to receive, investigate and pass on complaints alleging discrimination, to hold hearings and to subpoena witnesses.

What is the procedure of enforcement? An applicant or employee who feels that he has been the victim of an unlawful employment practice may file a verified complaint with the Commission in which he sets forth the facts. The Commission then makes a prompt investigation through one of its Commissioners, and if it is determined that probable cause exists, an attempt is made to end the unlawful practice by conference, conciliation and persuasion.

If this fails, the Commissioner may order the employer or organization charged to appear at a hearing before three members of the Commission excluding the member who made the investigation. If, at the hearing, the Commission finds that there has been an unlawful employment practice, it will issue an order requiring the offender to cease and desist and to right the wrong which has been committed, i.e. hire the person discriminated against. If no unlawful employment practice is found to have occurred, the complaint is dismissed. Review and enforcement of the Commission's orders is through the courts of the state.

What are the penalties under FEP? Willful violation of an order of the Commission or willfully resisting or impeding the Commission in its attempts to enforce the law is a misdemeanor punishable by a maximum of one year in prison or a maximum fine of $500 or both.

What groups are exempt from FEP? Social, fraternal, charitable, educational and religious associations--all organizations which are not organized for private profit--are specifically excluded from the law.

What may employers do if their employees refuse to work with persons of particular races or creeds? They may appeal to the Commission for relief, since the law forbids any person, whether employer or employee, to obstruct its enforcement.

Does FEP create a quota system in employment? No, a quota system is an unlawful employment practice under the law.

Nondiscrimination in Federal Employment and Related Activities

By Executive Order 11246 (1965), the federal government banned all discrimination in employment on federal jobs for reasons of race, creed, color or national origin. Enforcement of the order is in the hands of the Civil Service Commission and the Secretary of Labor. The order requires the head of each executive department and agency of the federal government to maintain a positive program of equal opportunity for all civilian employees and employment applicants. The Civil Service Commission is directed to review department and agency programs periodically to assure that the fair employment policies are carried out and to provide for prompt and impartial consideration of all complaints of discrimination.

In the Armed Forces, the government has sought with varying degrees of success to promote equal opportunity at least since 1948 when President Truman banned segregation in the services by executive order. The major continuing manifestations of discrimination exist in the promotional opportunities for Negroes to officer and higher ranking enlisted men's ratings. A Defense Department directive issued in 1963 authorized the creation of an office of Deputy Assistant Secretary for Civil Rights to try to deal with this problem. The same directive also ordered military commanders to oppose off-base discrimination against the men in their command. Since the passage of the Civil Rights Act of 1964, base commanders also are responsible for enforcing on behalf of military personnel the nondiscrimination provisions in relation to public accommodations, public facilities and education.

Discrimination on the part of government contractors and subcontractors is also forbidden by executive order. The various penalties for violation of the contractor's agreement made pursuant to the order include cancellation of the contract, institution of proceedings under Title VII of the 1964 Civil Rights Act and criminal proceedings against the contractor for the furnishing of false information to an agency of the government. An executive order also banned discrimination in federally assisted construction contracts.

THE FEDERAL EQUAL EMPLOYMENT STATUTE: Title VII of the 1964 Civil Rights Act is largely modeled on the states' FEP laws. It establishes the Equal Employment Opportunity Commission (EEOC) with powers to investigate and to attempt to conciliate complaints of discrimination in employment because of race, color, religion, sex or national origin. Coverage of the title extends to employers, public and private employment agencies, labor unions and joint labor-management apprenticeship or training programs. On July 2, 1967, the Act applied to employers with 50 or more persons and on July 2, 1968, to employers with 25 or more employees.

Not covered by the statute, however, are local, state, and federal agencies, government-owned corporations, Indian tribes, religious organizations where the employee is engaged in religious activities, and educational institutions where the employee performs work connected with the institution's educational activities.

In addition to its investigative and complaint conciliation functions, EEOC seeks to promote programs of voluntary compliance by employers and others affected by the Act. The Commission is also required to defer action on complaints for not less than 60 days in cases arising in states where enforceable fair employment practice laws exist.

When complaints are filed with the Commission, they are initially handled by the Commission's Compliance Division. The analysis section of the Division assigns complaints to the following categories: "probable jurisdiction"; "no jurisdiction"; "deferred for state action"; "returned for additional information." The "probable jurisdiction" complaints are assigned for investigation. The investigators first contact the complainant and his witnesses. They then serve the charged party with a copy of the charge and investigate the complaint. If it appears that the complaint has grounds, the Commission sends conciliators to attempt to resolve the complaint to the satisfaction of all parties concerned. If conciliation efforts fail, the complainant may then take his complaint to a United States District Court.

Title VII of the 1964 Civil Rights Act was (along with Title II banning discrimination in places of public accommodation) one of the most hotly debated portions of the Act and is the product of drastic compromise. Emulating, as it does, the state FEP laws, it has the essential weakness of those laws: the reliance on the slow, tortuous process of administrative action initiated by complaints and further extended by lengthy judicial processes. However, unlike many of the state commissions, EEOC lacks even the power to issue orders requiring cessation of unlawful employment practices. In this respect, it has less power than that usually given to federal regulatory agencies created under other kinds of federal statutes, e.g., the National Labor Relations Board (NLRB) or the Federal Trade Commission (FTC).

While bills filed in Congress in 1967 sought to strengthen the EEOC's powers by granting the Commission the right to subpoena and to issue court-enforcible cease and desist orders, the legislation was not adopted. The Civil Rights Act of 1968 protects workers in the exercise of their civil rights. Perhaps the most concrete step taken at the federal level, however, has been the filing by the Justice Department in April, 1969, of a suit against a major southern textile company, charging bias in employment and the rental of company housing. It was the first time the government had moved against segregated company-owned housing.

DISCRIMINATION FORBIDDEN ON PUBLIC WORKS: The following nine states forbid discrimination for reasons of race, color, or religion--Arizona, California, Colorado, Massachusetts, Minnesota, New Jersey, New York, Ohio, Pennsylvania. Similar legislation in Illinois, Indiana and Kansas prohibits discrimination on public works specifically for reasons of race or color, but probably embraces religious discrimination as well. Colorado extends the ban on discrimination to all private contractors retained for any work where public tax money is involved, and both Colorado and New York require an anti-discrimination clause to be included in contracts negotiated by the state with contractors. California, by constitutional amendment, now forbids the exclusion of Chinese from employment on public works.

Several states have additional legislation forbidding discrimination in employment on work that is in the public interest. Illinois, Nebraska, New Jersey and New York forbid discrimination in employment in defense work. New York forbids refusal by a public utility company to employ a person because of race, creed, color or national origin. Massachusetts forbids discrimination because of race, color or national origin by street railway companies owned or financially aided by the state. New York, Kansas and Nebraska have specific legislation forbidding discrimination in membership by labor organizations. Discrimination in relief for reasons of race, color or creed is forbidden in Illinois, Massachusetts, New York and Pennsylvania, for reasons of religion by New Jersey and for reasons of color by North Carolina.

It should be borne in mind that in those states where enforceable FEP laws have been enacted, these, in effect, include the narrower legislation dealing with public works, although such legislation remains on the books.

DISCRIMINATION FORBIDDEN IN PUBLIC SERVICE: Religious tests for public offices are specifically banned in 22 states --Alabama, Arkansas, Georgia, Indiana, Iowa, Kansas, Maine, Maryland, Minnesota, Missouri, Nebraska, New Jersey, Ohio, Oregon, Pennsylvania, Rhode Island, Tennessee, Texas, Utah, Washington, West Virginia, Wisconsin. Actually, under the Constitution, religious tests for public office would be illegal even in the absence of a specific law.

In the area of civil service, discrimination for reasons of religion is specifically forbidden in 13 states--California, Connecticut, Kansas, Maine, Massachusetts, Michigan, Minnesota, Nebraska, New Jersey, New York, Ohio, Pennsylvania, Wisconsin. Religious inquiry for civil service positions is forbidden in California, Illinois, Oregon, Pennsylvania and Wisconsin. Discrimination in civil service employment for reasons of race or color is specifically forbidden in six states which likewise forbid discrimination for reasons of religion--California, Connecticut, Illinois, Massachusetts, Michigan, New York. Michigan also forbids removals from or demotions in civil service for religious or racial reasons. Pennsylvania declares that an employee of the police department may not be removed for religious or racial reasons, and forbids exclusion from examination for employment in penal or correction institutions because of race or religious opinion.

In the area of public school appointments, discrimination for reasons of religion is forbidden in five states--California, Illinois, New Jersey, Wisconsin, Wyoming, and religious inquiry or test for such appointment is forbidden in eight states--California, Colorado, Idaho, Illinois, Iowa, Nebraska, New Mexico, New York. Discrimination in public school appointment for reasons of race or color is forbidden in California, New Jersey and Wisconsin. New Jersey also provides that dismissals from employment as principal or teacher, resulting from reduction in staff, shall not be based on race or religion.

DISCRIMINATION BECAUSE OF AGE: Legislation exists in twenty-three states and Puerto Rico forbidding discrimination because of age. The states are Alaska, California, Colorado, Connecticut, Delaware, Hawaii, Idaho, Indiana, Louisiana, Maine, Maryland, Massachusetts, Michigan, Nebraska, New Jersey, New York, North Dakota, Ohio, Oregon, Pennsylvania, Rhode Island, Washington and Wisconsin. The primary purpose of these statutes is to eliminate discrimination against older workers. They are usually applicable to workers between ages 40-65. While some of the laws apply to all private employment, most of them exempt such occupations as domestic servants, employment by a member of the family and by nonprofit charitable, religious or educational organizations.

Equal Opportunity in Education

As of May, 1954, the following states either compelled or expressly permitted segregation--Alabama, Delaware, Florida, Georgia, Kentucky, Louisiana, Maryland, Mississippi, Missouri, New Mexico, North Carolina, Oklahoma, South Carolina, Tennessee, Texas, West Virginia, Wyoming and the District of Columbia. In the famous School Segregation Cases (1954, 1955) the Supreme Court ruled compulsory segregation in public schools unconstitutional. School systems were ordered to end segregation "with all deliberate speed" and to move toward integration in a "systematic and effective" manner, within a "reasonable time."

As of October, 1963, New Mexico, Wyoming and Missouri had repealed their school segregation laws, and the District of Columbia had desegregated its public schools. At the present time, all of the remaining 14 southern and border states, some 1,141 school districts, have made at least some token progress toward desegregation.

But the intervening years have been marked with various forms of resistance to school desegregation. Most southern states soon after the second Brown decision in 1955, passed interposition resolutions. Two states, Arkansas and Mississippi, established State Sovereignty Commissions "to resist the usurpation of the rights and powers reserved to this state . . . by the Federal Government." Georgia and Alabama sent memorials to Congress protesting the illegality of the Brown decision. There was also the celebrated "Southern Manifesto" signed by all southern Congresmen and introduced in both houses. These things set the mood of defiance.

Virginia enacted a Pupil Placement Law designed to circumvent desegregation, but it was held to be unconstitutional (1957) and Arkansas laws which closed Little Rock high schools were likewise declared unconstitutional (1959). A Louisiana local-option law permitting the closing of public schools as an alternative to integration was held unconstitutional (1962), and a Tennessee law providing for "voluntary" school desegregation was characterized as "patently and manifestly unconstitutional" (1957). In Delaware, a grade-a-year desegregation plan was struck down and full integration ordered for the fall semester (1961).

The degree of resistance to desegregation, from the legal standpoint is perhaps best exemplified by actions in Virginia, all of which were set aside by the inexorable process of court application of the desegregation decision. In 1959, Virginia's State Supreme Court ruled that the state constitution barred closing individual schools in order to thwart desegregation, and in the same year a Federal District Court ruled the "massive resistance" laws unconstitutional. In 1961, the Federal District Court ruled that public funds may not be used to finance private schools for white students of Prince Edward County, as long as public schools were kept closed to avoid integration. A tragic commentary on the Prince Edward situation was a fact that for some three years Negro youngsters were virtually barred from educational opportunity. In 1962, the Court declared that schools of one county may not be closed to avoid compliance with court orders, while other public schools in the state remain open. And in 1963 the Supreme Court barred payment of state tuition grants to white private schools pending the Court's review of the Prince Edward school closing case. The following year, the Court ordered the County schools reopened. By this time, Negro children in Prince Edward County had been without public education for more than five years.

Elsewhere in the deep South, resistance frequently took the form of violence and terror, as distinguished from Virginia's effort to utilize legal measures to avoid desegregation. Mob violence occurred in Clinton, Tennessee; Mansfield, Texas and Little Rock, Arnaksas in 1956 and 1957. There was also violent opposition in Sturgis, Kentucky and Nashville, Tennessee. New Orleans made its contribution in 1960.

Despite the inexorable course of federal court decisions and sometimes forceful federal action to counter mob action, violence has not abated altogether. There was violence in Birmingham, Alabama, in September, 1963. A course of violent opposition commencing in September, 1963, and continuing into February, 1964, occurred in connection with desegregation of the schools in Macon County, Alabama. And in 1966, racial violence flared in Grenada, Mississippi, when white mobs attacked Negro children seeking to attend newly integrated facilities. 1970 has seen violence and death in Jackson, Mississippi.

Nor has the North been without its problems in this area. While 11 states forbid exclusion of or discrimination against students in public schools for reasons of race or color, and court action operates to invalidate segregation of students everywhere, the merging fact of the "neighborhood school" has created de facto segregation even where integration, as a matter of law, is not resisted. This has resulted in a legal focus on segregation in northern schools. An initial confrontation took place in New Rochelle, where a lower court order requiring the city to desegregate a gerrymandered, predominantly Negro school was affirmed by the Supreme Court. A similar legal battle was launched in Englewood, New Jersey.

In New York State, the State Education Commissioner ordered a racial census of all public schools in 1961 in a drive to eliminate de facto segregation. In 1963, this was followed up by an order to all school boards to take steps to correct racial imbalance in the public schools. In an initial test of the Commissioner's authority in Malverne, Long Island, a lower court refused to sustain the Commissioner's power, but it was later sustained by the New York Court of Appeals, though eventually limited by the Legislature.

Many northern school districts have become involved in the demands and counter-demands related to the bussing or transferring of students out of their neighborhoods in order to end de facto segregation. White parents have demonstrated, claiming that the civil rights of their children are infringed by programs designed to take children out of their neighborhoods in order to create integrated schools. Court battles on so-called "forced integration" are shaping up in a variety of northern metropolitan communities. New York has enacted an anti-bussing law, which has served as a model for Alabama, Georgia, Louisiana, South Carolina and Tennessee.

At the core of the problem in the North is whether a school board may constitutionally take race into account in order to relieve "racial imbalance." The majority judicial opinion is that they may but are not required to do so. This seems also to be the balance struck thus far by the Supreme Court, since it has refused to review two decisions holding that school boards have no duty (Gary, Indiana, and Kansas City, Kansas) as well as one holding that school boards may if they choose (New York City). Most of the voluntary action taken to ease racial imbalance has occurred in New Jersey, New York, Maryland and California. The New York law mentioned above does not specifically mention bussing, but it deprives the State Commissioner of Education of the authority to apply measures for dealing with racial imbalance in reluctant communities.

At the college level, state colleges fall within the Supreme Court's invalidation of "separate but equal" facilities. As a result, the laws requiring separate colleges for whites and Negroes while still on the books of some 15 states, are rendered null and void. While desegregation at the college level was accomplished in the Middle South with a minimum of organized resistance, the attempts to desegregate state universities in Alabama and Mississippi created national issues as the governors of both of these states set up their own authority against that of the federal government. Both states, however, finally yielded to federal authority, and in the face of citations for contempt and the threat of fines and prison sentences, the governors deferred.

At the same time, laws forbidding discrimination for reasons of race, color or creed in private colleges have now been enacted in the following states--Connecticut, Idaho, Illinois, Indiana, Massachusetts, Minnesota, New Jersey, New York, Pennsylvania, and Washington. Similar in conception to FEP laws, these laws are known as Fair Educational Practices laws, and, in effect, they are designed to bar the use of the "quota system" in governing the entry of minority group students into private colleges. Enforcement is through hearings and the issuance of cease and desist orders, and in general, the state commissions set up under FEP have been given jurisdiction and authority over the administration of Fair Educational Practices laws.

The most significant recent developments in the school desegregation area have occured as a consequence of the passage of the 1964 Civil Rights Act. Under the Act, the Attorney General is authorized to bring school desegregation suits in the name of the United States upon receiving written complaints from parents in local communities stating that their children are being deprived of the equal protection of the laws by the local school officials. When the Attorney General believes the complaint is meritorious and certifies that the signer or signers are unable, in his judgment, to initiate and maintain legal proceedings, he may commence the action. Additionally, the Attorney General is now authorized to intervene in school desegregation cases initiated by private individuals.

But certainly the most far-reaching effect of the 1964 Civil Rights Act on school discrimination is that of Title VI of the Act and the guidelines adopted by the United States Office of Education for determining when a school board is in compliance with the Act's strictures against racial segregation in the schools. These guidelines, promulgated in 1965 and revised in 1966, require--as a condition for continued receipt of federal funds--that school officials implement desegregation plans designed to eliminate discrimination in all aspects of a school system's operation, e.g., pupil assignment and transfer, faculty placement, school construction plans, extra-curricular activities, etc. Fed-

107

eral appellate courts in the deep South have adopted the guide-lines as "minimum standards" for determining the appropriate relief in school desegregation cases but have made it clear that the courts retain primary responsibility for implementing the Brown decision.

Equal Opportunity in Housing

There have been a variety of approaches on the federal and state levels to the problem of discrimination in housing. To date, none has been markedly successful. Probably the earliest was the legislative approach of the first Reconstruction Civil Rights Act (Act of 1866) which contained a provision that "all citizens of the United States shall have the same right, in every State and Territory, as is enjoyed by white citizens thereof to inherit, purchase, lease, sell, hold and convey real and personal property." This provision has not been repealed and is a part of present law (42 U.S.C. paragraph 1986). Again, the problem with respect to its effective application was that of whether it is a restraint on the action of individuals and private groups or for government only. The problem was resolved for fair housing in the 1968 Civil Rights Act.

Housing built under federal government programs or with federal assistance must as a matter of fairly recent governmental policy be made available to all on a nondiscriminatory basis. Executive Order No. 11063 promulgated by President Kennedy in 1962 directed all departments and agencies of the government dealing with housing to take "all action necessary and appropriate to prevent discrimination because of race, color, creed or national origin." This order affected the three major housing programs of the federal government: the mortgage insurance programs of the Federal Housing Administration (FHA) and the Veteran's Administration (VA), the subsidized low-income public housing program administered by the Public Housing Administration (PHA) and the urban renewal program established by the Housing Act of 1949. All these programs are now administered under the overall authority of the Department of Housing and Urban Development (HUD) which was added to the cabinet in 1966. With passage of Title VI of the 1964 Civil Rights Act, Congress has in effect elevated the President's Executive Order to a widely applicable rule with more extensive coverage of activities related to housing. The Civil Rights Act of 1968 in effect outlaws nationally discrimination in rental and sales of residential quarters.

There have also been some judicially created restrictions on housing discrimination. The earliest of these dealt with municipal racial zoning ordinances which the Supreme Court declared unconstitutional in 1917 and again in 1927 and 1930. Restrictive covenents have been outlawed (see below); the Supreme Court has held that they may not be enforced by injunctions seeking specific performance nor may a person get money damages for breach of the terms of the covenant.

State efforts in the field have been primarily--if not exclusively--legislative. The Model Anti-discrimination Act (supra, p.78) contains proposed provisions in sections 601-607 dealing with discrimination in real property transactions to include transactions by owners, real estate brokers and salesmen and financing institutions. The subject matter areas to which existing state laws extend are summarized below.

PUBLIC HOUSING: Discrimination for race, creed or color is now forbidden in 17 states--Alaska, California, Colorado, Connecticut, Illinois, Indiana, Massachusetts, Michigan, Minnesota, New Hampshire, New Jersey, New York, Ohio, Oregon, Pennsylvania, Rhode Island, and Wisconsin. Laws also exist in Puerto Rico, the Virgin Islands and the District of Columbia.

PUBLICLY ASSISTED HOUSING: Discrimination for race, creed or color is now forbidden in 14 states--Alaska, California, Colorado, Connecticut, Massachusetts, Michigan, Minnesota, New Hampshire, New Jersey, New York, Ohio, Oregon, Pennsylvania, and Washington. Puerto Rico, the Virgin Islands and the District of Columbia also have statutes covering this kind of housing.

URBAN RENEWAL: Redevelopment housing--the replacement of a slum area with a newly-planned community--is closely associated with publicly assisted housing. Federal urban renewal regulations forbid the drawing of redevelopment project boundaries in a discriminatory way and require representation in the planning of these projects by members of the minority community being displaced. Failure to comply with these regulations (and those requiring the provision of adequate relocation facilities and resources) may result in the withholding of funds for renewal projects by the Housing and Urban Development Department as occurred in 1967 in Pulaski, Tennessee.

The states with laws forbidding discrimination in the selection of tenants for renewal projects are: Alaska, California, Colorado, Connecticut, Indiana, Massachusetts, Michigan, Minnesota, Montana, New Hampshire, New Jersey, New York, Ohio, Oregon, Pennsylvania, Washington and Wisconsin. The District of Columbia, Puerto Rico, and the Virgin Islands also have such laws.

MORTGAGE LENDERS: Colorado, Connecticut, Massachusetts, Minnesota, New Jersey, New York and Pennsylvania--a total of 7 states--bar discrimination by mortgage lenders.

PRIVATE HOUSING: Fair Housing Practices laws--again, in the mould of FEP--have been enacted in 16 states, the District of Columbia, Puerto Rico, and the Virgin Islands. Alaska, California, Colorado, Connecticut, Indiana, Massachusetts, Michigan, Minnesota, New Hampshire, New Jersey, New York, Ohio, Oregon, Pennsylvania, Rhode Island and Wisconsin are the states. In Connecticut, Massachusetts, and New York, the only exemptions are owner-occupied one- or two-family dwellings. The Supreme Court has upheld constitutionality by refusing to review.

The City of New York in 1957 adopted the first ordinance in the country barring racial or religious discrimination in private housing. In 1961, the ordinance was broadened to include 95% of all dwellings. Enforcement is simplified. The Commission on Human Rights is authorized to seek restraining orders barring disposal of property pending outcome of proceedings. At least 17 municipal ordinances barring discrimination in private housing have been enacted since the beginning of 1963. Some of the cities included are Philadelphia, Pittsburgh, Schenectady, N.Y.,

Albuquerque, N.M., Oberlin and Toledo, Ohio, Chicago, Washington, D.C., St. Louis, New London, Conn., Peoria, Illinois, Ann Arbor and Grand Rapids, Michigan, Duluth, Minnesota, Madison, Wisconsin and New Haven, Conn.

The problem involved in fair housing legislation on both the state and municipal level is that of the lack of vigorous administrative enforcement. Too often state commissions have de-emphasized the obtaining of housing accommodations for persons who have been denied housing because of their race or color but have contented themselves with obtaining assurances from law violators not to discriminate in the future. The New York Commission, the oldest in the field, was charged in 1967 in a petition and complaint filed with them by the NAACP Legal Defense Fund with some specific derelictions with respect to their enforcement practices. The Commission was charged with (1) delaying action on complaints, (2) failing to seek court injunctions on behalf of complainants, (3) offering conciliation terms which fail to safeguard complainants' rights to future available housing, (4) failing to take steps against multiple violators and (5) failing to notify complainants of developments in their cases pertinent to their efforts to obtain housing. Lack of appropriate administrative initiative in enforcement has blunted the effect of fair housing legislation despite its proliferation.

Other problems have arisen from widespread opposition to fair housing legislation. Though opponents of these measures have not been successful in the courts, they have met with greater success in the public forum and at the polls. In recent years, opposition to fair housing laws spearheaded by the real estate industry, has contributed to the defeat of ordinances in Berkeley, California, Tacoma and Seattle, Washington, and Akron and Dayton, Ohio. An anti-fair housing law was adopted in Detroit in 1964. And in California, the voters in the November, 1964, election adopted "Proposition 14," a constitutional amendment repealing existing state fair housing laws and prohibiting the enactment of similar legislation in the future. However, the California Supreme Court subsequently overruled the voters' action and has been sustained by the U.S. Supreme Court.

RESTRICTIVE COVENANTS: The racial restrictive covenants in a deed or lease by which land cannot be sold or leased to persons of particular religious or racial groups was declared unenforceable by the Supreme Court in 1948. California (1961) and New York (1962) enacted legislation voiding racial and ethnic restrictive covenants in real property deeds, and Minnesota has had such a statute on its books since 1919.

REGULATION OF REAL ESTATE BROKERS: The Connecticut Commission on Civil Rights, the Attorney-Generals of California, Massachusetts and Oregon, and the Superior Court of Washington, have ruled that real estate brokers are covered by state laws barring discrimination in services offered to the public. Real estate licensing authorities in New York and Pennsylvania have barred racial or religious discrimination by real estate salesmen and brokers in sales or rentals and forbid efforts to stimulate panic selling in real estate transactions.

Two cases, one decided by the Supreme Court of New Jersey, the other by the Supreme Court of Indiana, have prohibited the exclusion on racial grounds of real estate brokers in those states from membership in the brokers' multilist organization or from access to the multi-listing pursuant to which the listings of properties on the housing market are consolidated and distributed to brokers. At present, a suit is pending in a federal district court in Pennsylvania brought on by an antitrust theory, to require the Greater Pittsburgh Multilist Association to admit Negro brokers.

A lawsuit has also been brought against the Akron, Ohio, Area Board of Realtors on an antitrust theory to prohibit the restraint of trade involved in denying access of minorities to the housing market. The Ohio district court (federal) dismissed the case on the ground that the activities of the defendants were local in nature and did not "occur within the flow of interstate commerce." The case has been appealed to the United States Court of Appeals for the Sixth Circuit.

Equal Opportunity to Health and Welfare Services

The problem of discrimination in medical facilities--public and private hospitals, custodial institutions, health centers, nursing homes, clinics and mental institutions--received scant attention prior to 1963. Most southern states require racial segregation to these institutions by law; in the absence of a specific legislative provision, custom prevailed. In addition, prior to 1964 federal law sanctioned racial discrimination in state hospitals. The Hill-Burton Act of 1946 providing for the channeling of federal funds for the construction of state hospitals authorized the Surgeon General of the United States to permit state authorities to establish separate hospital facilities for separate population groups, i.e., "separate-but-equal."

Then in November, 1963, the landmark case of Simkins v. Moses H. Cone Memorial Hospital was decided by the United States Court of Appeals for the Fourth Circuit. The court held that (1) acceptance of federal funds channeled to the states under a joint federal-state scheme made the accepting hospitals subject to the provisions of the Fifth and Fourteenth Amendments prohibiting discrimination and (2) the "separate-but-equal" provision of the Hill-Burton Act and the regulations promulgated pursuant thereto were unconstitutional. The Supreme Court, by declining to review this decision left it intact. This action by our highest court was properly read as an endorsement of the Fourth Circuit's holding.

Since the Simkins case, a number of federal courts have enjoined public and private medical institutions from continuing racial segregation and other discriminatory practices including discrimination in professional staffing practices. Discrimination in professional medical and dental associations has also been outlawed by court decisions in North Carolina and Georgia.

Among the states outlawing discriminating in health care by statute are Arizona, Massachusetts, New Hampshire, New Jersey, New Mexico, New York and Pennsylvania. The California public accommodations law has been interpreted to include health facilities. Section 401(b)(4) of the Model Anti-discrimination Act bars discrimination in a "dispensary, clinic, hospital, convalescent home, or other institution for the infirm."

Title VI of the Civil Rights Act of 1964 prohibits discrimination "under any program or activity receiving federal financial assistance." The sanction for continued discrimination is termination of federal funds. Regulations have been issued under Title VI by the Department of Health, Education and Welfare stating the conditions for continued elibibility of state health programs for federal money, but to date, very little has been accomplished by administrative action toward eradicating discrimination in health care despite the sweeping mandate of the legislation. This is true even though under the federal Medicare program established by Congress in 1965 as a part of the national Social Security System, Medicare insurance payments are conditioned upon hospitals meeting a variety of health and safety requirements and discouraging improper and unnecessary utilization of services and facilities thus placing few state medical facilities beyond the reach of the nondiscrimination provisions of Title VI.

WELFARE SERVICES: Discrimination in this area occurs chiefly through a combination of arbitrary state and local welfare rules and policies for determining eligibility for assistance, administrative regulations as the "substitute parent" or "man-in-the-house" rules adopted in many states (no eligibility for welfare assistance if mother of dependent children has "improper" relationship with a man) and the "employable mother" or "suitable work" rule (continued eligibility depends on mother seeking suitable employment) have been used to fit the notions of welfare administrators as to who are deserving poor. These and similar types of rules were attached in a complaint filed by the NAACP Legal Defense Fund with the Department of Health, Education and Welfare in 1966. The employable mother rule has also been challenged as racially discriminatory in a federal injunction in Georgia with success.

Some cities, notably New York, Baltimore and Detroit, have suspended their former practice of conducting early morning "visits" by welfare investigators to the homes of welfare recipients for the purpose of discovering whether a mother on welfare has a "forbidden" relationship with a man. Revised regulations of the Bureau of Family Services of the Department of Health, Education and Welfare issued in March, 1966, and effective July 1, 1967, provides that state policies for determining eligibility for welfare assistance must not violate the individual's privacy, personal dignity or constitutional rights.

WOMEN'S RIGHTS: For an expanded discussion of women and their rights as a special victim of discrimination, especially in the area of employment, the reader is advised to see The Legal Status of Women in the Legal Almanac Series.

114

APPENDIX A

First Ten Amendments (Adopted in 1791)

Amendment (I)

Congress shall make no law respecting an establishment of religion, or prohibiting the free exercise thereof; or abridging the freedom of speech, or of the press; or the right of the people peaceably to assemble, and to petition the Government for a redress of grievances.

Amendment (II)

A well regulated Militia, being necessary to the security of a free State, the right of the people to keep and bear Arms, shall not be infringed.

Amendment (III)

No Soldier shall, in time of peace be quartered in any house, without the consent of the Owner, nor in time of war, but in a manner to be prescribed by law.

Amendment (IV)

The right of the people to be secure in their persons, houses, papers, and effects, against unreasonable searches and seizures, shall not be violated, and no Warrants shall issue, but upon probable cause, supported by Oath or affirmation, and particularly describing the place to be searched, and the persons or things to be seized.

Amendment (V)

No person shall be held to answer for a capital or otherwise infamous crime, unless on a presentment or indictment of a Grand Jury, except in cases arising in the land or naval forces, or in the Militia, when in actual service in time of War or public danger; nor shall any person be subject for the same offense to be twice put in jeopardy of life or limb; nor shall be compelled in any criminal case to be a witness against himself, nor be deprived of life, liberty, or property, without due process of law; nor shall private property be taken for public use, without just compensation.

Amendment (VI)

In all criminal prosecutions, the accused shall enjoy the right to a speedy and public trial, by an impartial jury of the State and district wherein the crime shall have been committed, which district shall have been previously ascertained by law, and to be informed of the nature and cause of the accusation; to be confronted with the witnesses against him; to have compulsury process for obtaining witnesses in his favor, and to have the Assistance of Counsel for his defense.

Amendment (VII)

In Suits at common law, where the value in controversy shall exceed twenty dollars, the right of trial by jury shall be preserved, and no fact tried by a jury, shall be otherwise re-examined in any Court of the United States, than according to the rules of the common law.

Amendment (VIII)

Excessive bail shall not be required, nor excessive fines imposed, nor cruel and unusual punishments inflicted.

Amendment (IX)

The enumeration in the Constitution, of certain rights, shall not be construed to deny or disparage others retained by the people.

Amendment (X)

The powers not delegated to the United States by the Constitution, nor prohibited by it to the States, are reserved to the States respectively, or to the people.

Amendment (XIII)

Section 1. Neither slavery nor involuntary servitude, except as a punishment for crime whereof the party shall have been duly convicted, shall exist within the United States, or any place subject to their jurisdiction.

Section 2. Congress shall have power to enforce this article by appropriate legislation.

Amendment (XIV)

Section 1. All persons born or naturalized in the United States, and subject to the jurisdiction thereof, are citizens of the United States and of the State wherein they reside. No State shall make or enforce any law which shall abridge the privileges or immunities of citizens of the United States; nor shall any State deprive any person of life, liberty, or property without due process of law; nor deny to any person within its jurisdiction the equal protection of the laws.

Amendment (XV)

Section 1. The right of citizens of the United States to vote shall not be denied or abridged by the United States or by any State on account of race, color, or previous condition of servitude.

Section 2. The Congress shall have power to enforce this article by appropriate legislation.

The right of citizens of the United States to vote shall not be denied or abridged by the United States or by any State on account of sex.

Congress shall have power to enforce this article by appropriate legislation.

AMENDMENT XXVI

Section 1. The right of citizens of the United States, who are 18 years of age or older, to vote shall not be denied or abridged by the United States or by any State on account of age.

Section 2. The Congress shall have power to enforce this article by appropriate legislation.

Provisions from the Original Constitution

ARTICLE I

Section 9 . . .
2. The privilege of the writ of habeas corpus shall not be suspended, unless when in cases of rebellion or invasion the public safety may require it.

3. No bill of attainder or ex post facto law shall be passed.

Section 10 . . .
1. No State shall... pass any bill of attainder, ex post facto law, or law impairing the obligation of contracts...

ARTICLE III

Section 2 . . .
3. The trial of all crimes, except in cases of impeachment, shall be by jury . . .

Section 3.

1. Treason against the United States shall consist only in levying war against them, or in adhering to their enemies, giving them aid and comfort. No Person shall be convicted of treason unless on the testimony of two witnesses to the same overt act, or on confession in open court.

ARTICLE IV

Section 2.

1. The citizens of each State shall be entitled to all privileges and immunities of citizens in the several States.

ARTICLE VI

3. . no religious test shall ever be required as a qualification to any office or public trust under the United States.

INDEX

Advice of counsel, 63-65
Alien and Sedition Acts
    of 1798, 33, 35
Alien Registration Act
    (1940 - Smith Act),
    35-37, 39
Alien subversion, 42-43
Anti-Busing Law, 106
Bill of Rights, 47-48,
    58, 67-68, 70
"Blue Ribbon" jury, 62-63
Censorship, 13-14
    books and magazines, 16-17
    civil and criminal penalties
      for, 23-25
    mail, 20-21
    motion pictures, 18-19
    on the federal level, 19-21
    press, 22-23
    radio and TV, 19-20
    theatrical production, 15-16
Civil liberties and civil rights,
    definition and distinction,
    ix-x
Civil rights, 81-114
    enforcement of federal
      criminal statutes, 86-89
    federal government, role
      of, 65-77, 81-93
    states and civil rights, 93-99
Civil Rights Acts
    (1875), 82
    (1957), 84-91
    (1960), 85
    (1964), 84-85, 91, 100, 107
    (1968), 85

Disclosure requirements for
    subversives, 39-40
Discrimination forbidden,
    age, 103
    jury selection, 88
    public service, 102-103
    public works, 101
    (See "Equal Opportunity" below)
Disorderly conduct, see
    Punishment of breach of the peace
Double jeopardy, 54-56
Due process, 58-61
Eavesdropping, 52-53
Equal access to services and
    accommodations, 94-95
Equal Employment Opportunity
    Commissin (EEOC), 100
Equal opportunity in education,
    103-108
Equal opportunity in employment,
    97-103
Equal opportunity in housing,
    108-112
    private housing, 110-111
    public housing, 104-110
Equal opportunity to health and
    welfare services, 112-114
Espionage Act of 1917, 34-36
Fair Employment Practices
    (FEP) legislation, 97-102, 107
Fairness Doctrine, 19-20
Fair trial, 58-61
Federal Anti-Riot Act, 23, 30
Federal Equal Employment
    statute, 100-102
Federal Immunity Statute
    (1954), 58

Federal Peacetime Sedition Act, 35-37

Freedom of the press, 22-23

Freedom of religion, 1-11

Government aid to education, 7-11

Habeas corpus, 48-49

Indictments by grand jury, 53-54

Law and Order, 29-31

Legislative investigations into subversion, 46-47

Libel, 22-24

Licensing, 26-28

"No knock" legislation, 69

Obscenity, 13-18

Omnibus Crime Control Act, 69

Personal liberty, guarantees of, 47-71

Police power regulations v. freedom of expression, 25-28

Prayers and Bible reading, 4-6

Prior restraints, see Licensing

Preventive detention, 70

Privilege against self-incrimination, 56-58

Punishment of breach of peace or disorderly conduct, 27-28

Real estate brokers, regulation of, 112

Religion and the schools, 4-11

aid to education, 7-11

released time, 6

religious holiday observances, 7

Restrictive covenants, 111-112

Right to counsel during custodial interrogation, 65-66

Right to vote, 89-93

Rights after conviction of crime, 68-70

post-conviction remedies, 67-68

prisoner remedies, 69

Searches and seizures, 49-52

Sedition and subversion, 33-34

war measures, 34-35

Peacetime Sedition Act, 35-37

Segregation, 95-97

and breach of peace, 96-97

"State Action" doctrine, 83

State sedition laws, 37-39

Subversive Activities Control Act (1950), 30-31

Travel restrictions, 41-42

Trial and defense, 61-70

Trial by jury, 61-63

Urban renewal, 109-110

Voting Rights Act of 1965, 92-93

Wiretapping, 52-53